The Competent Organization

Books by Lee Thayer:

Leadership: Thinking, Being, Doing

The Field Guide Companion to Leadership: Thinking, Being, Doing

How Executives Fail (New and Revised Edition)

The Good Leader

Leaders and Leadership: Searching for Wisdom in All the Right Places

Leadership Virtuosity: A Trove of Virtuoso Ideas

How Leaders Think

The Myth of "The Leader"

Explaining Things: Inventing Ourselves and Our Worlds

Communication! A Radically New Approach to Life's Most Perplexing Problem

The Competent Organization

Lee Thayer

To order additional copies of this book, contact:
Xlibris Corporation
1-888-795-4274
www.Xlibris.com
Orders@Xlibris.com
104558

CONTENTS

Introduction:

Appreciating the *Concept* of Competence

There has been a fair amount of talk about the competence of people—or the lack thereof—in our recent past. But we seem to be seeing less and less of it in our civilization.

There has been little said about the competence of *organizations*. And yet that is what we want. That is what we need.

People may be trained to offer the cliché, "Have a nice day." This is usually offered in a desultory way and in lieu of actually making it a nice day for the person who is bombarded by this affront.

Walk off the plane or out of the store after you have been treated rudely or indifferently and you are likely to hear it. The worse you have been treated, the more likely you are to hear it.

This is more than simple hypocrisy. It dehumanizes everyone involved.

Like people in general, the more incompetent the organization the more it will spend and the more effort it will make to convince the customer or the client otherwise.

Or the patient: You are likely to buy no more than ten or fifteen *minutes* of the physician's time for a hundred dollars or so. And this may be after an hour's wait. That's because, as they are wont to say, "We care."

What does it mean to be competent in any interaction? What would it feel like to be dealt with competently by *any* person or *any* organization?

What would be the consequences for our civilization of dealing with other people competently? What would be the impact on our civilization to be dealt with competently by every organization you come in contact with?

It would be huge, obviously. And it would be for the good, obviously. But as the old saying goes, "No snowflake in an avalanche feels responsible." We are all controlled by convention.

There is no collective solution.

We may have good intentions. We may *mean* well. But when it comes down to performance, we are more likely to say and do and think and feel and have what is a la mode. What's in fashion is almost always more powerful than what's right.

Every relationship is a sort of organization. It gets institutionalized, even bureaucratized. Over time, it evolves its own culture—replete with its own prescriptions and proscriptions. Habits and routines rule the day. People in relationships are more likely to unconsciously serve their habits and routines (and the culture that evolves out of how they have treated one another) than they are to serve their own best self-interests.

People may think they have purposes in life. But what *has them* are the habits and routines that they have evolved over time.

People may have said at one time, with a purpose in mind, "I love you." But that too often comes to be said without any real meaning, without any real feeling.

Organizations evolve mainly by imitation. They become what is *possible* in the world of the conventions and fashions in which they exist. Our cultures—from those of a simple relationship to a global organization like the Catholic Church—lead us. We follow, not where we ought to go, but where our beliefs take us.

So those within the culture are following the dictates of that culture. Those who might want to have dealings with that culture are captive to a different culture. Often the two are not compatible. Rarely are they synergistic.

Our destiny comes from the machinations of the cultures we belong to, and from the machinations required to deal with other cultures.

If you have ever tried to do something by following the directions provided by a manufacturer or a distributor, you were much aware that you and the person who wrote the directions lived in two very different cultures.

If you have ever been the victim of someone trying to change your basic beliefs, you know how irritating and how unlikely this is to happen. If you have ever tried to change someone else's wrongheaded beliefs, you know how frustrating and unlikely it is that you would ever be successful.

The best exemplar would be that of trying to convince someone who hates you to love you. This is the prototype for much of the conflict going on in the world today.

Cultural—even occupational beliefs and values—are irrational. They are not very subject to rational arguments. That's where the rub comes in.

Palliatives are always rational. The problems that humans and societies create are not.

An irrational problem cannot be solved by rational means.

We have a long history of wars and all kinds of mistreatment of one another to demonstrate that.

In this book, I have no intention of taking on such a huge and complex problem as geopolitical conflict. We have an endless supply of "experts" who are ready, willing, and questionably able to take that on.

What I do intend to do is to examine in the most basic way what it would mean to compose and maintain a competent *organization*. And one that serves the best interests of all of its stakeholders, from its employees and customers to the communities it impacts and even the larger economy.

By definition, a competent organization is *good for* all who function in it, and all who have or would have dealings with it.

For the most part, we have not thought about organizations in this way.

It's well past time we did so.

This book will be of inestimable value to all readers who have encounters with organizations of any sort or size. It will enable readers to accurately assess the performance of those organizations. And, fortunately, it will enable them to do something about it.

This book will also be of inestimable value to all of those who write about or talk about organizations—journalists, critics, and book writers alike.

Mostly, however, this book will be of inestimable value conceptually and practically to those who create, manage, or lead organizations they intend to be competent.

As my readers well know, there is no one-size-fits-all recipe for making great, or high-performance, or even competent organizations. The most influential people in organizations vary greatly in personality, stamina, and imagination. The histories of those organizations vary greatly, as often also their cultures.

And people are people. They are never interchangeable with respect to imposed procedures, like two grains of salt.

The CEOs of organizations typically want to know how to "do it." Whether they can "do it" or not depends ultimately upon whether they did it or not.

There are no recipes. But there are basic principles.

This book does not attempt to provide you with a recipe for how you can make a competent organization. But it does tell you how you need to *think about* what needs thinking about in order to create a competent organization.

That is what leaders do. They begin with what they are trying to accomplish and then invent a way to get there.

We start by examining in fine detail what constitutes individual **competence**. We follow that by translating those criteria for the smallest organization—a relationship—on to larger and larger organizations.

Large or small, the principles remain the same. The tools you may find useful to deploy to achieve a competent **organization** we take up in Part III of the book. Thus equipped, you can figure out for yourself how the unique person *you* are can do it. The unique person you are is always the critical variable.

There we will consider the fundamental prerequisites for any and all competent organizations.

Finally, in the last part of this book, we will look back to see what we have learned. And we will consider again what it takes for any leader to be able to implement those principles in his or her organization.

The star by which we will navigate throughout is the *ideal*. If you don't aim for the ideal, you will arrive at the mediocre, the run-of-the-mill.

That is the premier lesson required for making competent organizations.

If you don't overshoot, you will undershoot.

PART I

Real competence is widely misunderstood in our society. If we are to grasp the idea of the competence of organizations rightly, we need to have a deeper and more real-world understanding of individual competence.

The following chapter addresses the concept of competence itself. This is followed by three chapters that explore in the thorough detail you will need to best think about individual competence.

One needs to think deeply about these several criteria. The reader needs to internalize these understandings. They are of little value on the printed page. They are of great value once they become a part of your everyday thinking and actions.

To best understand the competent organization, you must first have a thorough understanding of *competence* itself, then of what constitutes individual competence.

The competent organization requires more than individual competence. But it requires individual competence as a foundation.

The analogies will serve us well. The competent organization is somewhat more complex. But how competence is best perceived and attributed is similar.

Leaders know it is on this foundation that they have to build great—or even more competent—organizations.

1.   On Competence

In all of our waking hours with other people, we are necessarily engaged in playing a role. It may be a chosen role. Or it may be a role imposed by others or by the culture(s) which we inhabit.

In the first case, we have to play the role of the moment in a way that wins over others to our purposes. In the second, we must play the role to the expectations of others, or of the culture.

Competence in general refers to whether or not we play those roles more than or less than adequately. We will be judged. We will judge our own performance. Others will judge our performance. The criteria applied are the baseline for the range of competence we choose to or are called upon to perform.

We will be judged as playing our multifarious roles of the day and of our lives from acceptably to superbly.

That is the range of *competence*—from acceptably adequate to superlatively.

To be competent means that we have passed muster with ourselves and with others relative to our performance of the roles we play.

There are (in someone's view) competent children and incompetent children. There are competent parents and incompetent parents. There are competent husbands and wives, and some who aren't.

There are friends and acquaintances we consider competent, and some we don't. There are competent teachers and physicians and politicians and plumbers, and some who are judged not to be competent.

There are competent CEOs as judged, and there are those who are judged to be incompetent.

Similarly, there are competent organizations and incompetent organizations—as they are judged. They range from barely adequate to what may be judged as "the best." Sometimes, however, "the best" is merely the least worst of the sample.

There are public and there are folkloristic judgments. They use different criteria. Some are expert opinion dressed up to appear objective. But there is no real objectivity involved.

We have not, in fact, known how to measure in any valid or reliable way the competence of organizations. There are expert rankings. And there are expert assessments. Sometimes these are based on polls. But the results often differ.

As users of organizations of all types, we have had no valid way of assessing their competence. We may not know exactly how to do it. But we know incompetence when we experience it. And we know by comparison competence when we rarely encounter it.

We formulate an opinion based on our experiences. We check these out with the people we most often talk to. If they agree, we feel confident in our judgments. If they don't, then we will likely conclude that *they* are simply wrong.

That's part of the dilemma in trying to ascertain the competence of organizations. The other part of it is even more challenging.

It is that an organization may be competent, but not actually be good for us or for society in the long run. Or, an organization may be incompetent, but still make a positive contribution to our own or our society's long term interests.

Hitler's regime was competent. But the results were anything but laudatory (except for certain people at the time).

Gandhi's "organization" was largely ad hoc. He had disciples, just as did the partly historical, partly legendary Jesus. It was the disciples who did the heavy lifting. Still, we judged the results in both cases to be to the long-term benefit of certain classes of people.

Dictatorships can actually be good for their people and for their societies. Democratically-elected leaders can actually be bad for their people and the future of their societies.

What this makes clear is that competence in and of itself does not necessarily lead to good ends. There have been criminals who were more competent as criminals than the detectives who were trying to catch them were as detectives. Sometimes the bad guys win.

Incompetent parents are in general better at molding incompetent children than are competent parents. A competent physician does not necessarily have a better record than an incompetent physician.

When it comes to organizations:

- An organization can do everything right but sometimes fail.
- An organization can do everything wrong but sometimes succeed.

What this suggests is very important: *Competence does not guarantee success. There are always other variables at play.*

It happens that some organizations have very poor competitors and therefore seem to be succeeding. How good a football team looks may depend upon who they're playing.

If the audience members of a symphony concert are especially incompetent as consumers of music, the orchestra could never play at the level of which it may be capable. Great lovers bring out the best in one another. If one is actually incompetent in his or her role, the other cannot appear to be competent.

The reasons even the cleverest formulas do not work is that they are necessarily rational. But the world of people and economics and the weather are often irrational. In a comprehensibly bad economy, there will be no stand-outs. There they all look bad.

It bears repeating: **Competence does not guarantee success.**

It is probably always a necessary condition. But it is never a sufficient condition.

There are always other factors at play in the real world. Alexander the Great amassed the largest empire in the world up to that time. But that alone did not guarantee its continuation. That would have required competencies that he did not seem to have.

No one remains "number one" for long. Ask Tiger Woods. Ask any especially-successful CEO who leaves to take up that role somewhere else. They seem to fail more often than succeed.

What history makes clear is that it is not alone the competence of the leader that makes an organization successful—*or not.*

Yet there is a way of *conceptualizing* competence that minimizes the effects of those other variables while optimizing the probabilities of a positive outcome.

The answer lies in how we define competence. For that will determine how we evaluate it and how we enact it in practice.

There is another distinction of fundamental importance. You may have the best player in the country on your basketball team, but that does not guarantee a winning season. You could, in fact, have the *five* best players in the country on your team, but that still would not guarantee that you would garner the most wins over the season.

Individual competence does not predict to collective performance.

A competent organization requires competent people in every role, as we shall see. But there is something more that matters greatly in any 2-person or n-person organization.

If it is the collective that matters, then competence becomes partly a matter of competence at making the *collective* successful. It makes a great deal of difference whether the individuals are in it for their own purposes or whether they are there to make the organization successful.

If spouses compete for being the MVP of a marriage, for example, one or the other may "win." But the marriage loses.

The competence of an organization does not depend upon its star player, not even its "leader." The leader, like the spouse, may make his or her unique contribution. But the competence of the organization depends upon many factors beyond the competence of the individuals involved, as every great leader has known.

It depends upon how the organization is created, what it is *for*, and how it is nurtured by the competencies of all of those who comprise it. What is a marriage *for*? What is a corporation *for*? What is any organization at all *for*?

An organization can exist without conscious commitment to this ideal—without any real cognizance of what this organization is *for*.

But it will never be a fully competent organization.

To the extent that spouses do not know—or care—what their organization is *for* will suffer an impoverished relationship. And they will thus suffer an impoverished life.

To the extent that employees do not know what their organization is *for* will have at best half-lives at work. They may try to compensate for that half-life at work by their leisure pursuits. But even that may be impoverishing. They do not know what those leisure pursuits are *for*.

Whatever the reasons given: To *avoid* being a maker of good and worthy organizations is to lose out on what constitutes the real and lasting meaning of life itself.

People who belong to a *community* live longer, are healthier, and have more quality of life than their counterparts who have been led to believe it's all about *them*.

The meaning of life is bound up in what we do in it, and for what purpose.

Apart from the endless chattering of academics—there is no such thing as *competence* apart from the cause to which it is devoted. We learn to get by in a small world of like people, and then die a little daily.

In this sense, *competence* is the source of a meaningful life.

Show me a person who is not very good at *anything*, and I'll show you a person who is privately miserable—miserable because he or she is living a life that is pointless.

Competence is more than a set of skills. It is the source of any real life, individual or collective.

Most people tend to assume that they are more competent than they actually are.

This may be no more than what has been referred to as "personality armor." People want to make a good impression until accepted. So they may profess to themselves and others more competence than they really command.

It is minimally self-deception. The attempt to deceive others may end up being problematic.

It becomes problematic when it is time to deliver.

The distance between professing competence and delivering it is a long and often arduous apprenticeship. It is a path many would like to avoid. It's far easier to profess competence than it is to deliver it.

It is usually those who are themselves less than competent who accept the pretense. Once initiated, it is a bit like mutual blackmail.

One measure of a worthy person is that they know what they are capable of, and what they are not capable of. They do not take on assignments that exceed their competencies. This is extremely valuable. Not knowing one's limitations is what's important. It is more important than the ensuing performance itself.

People can develop new or greater competencies. But once any person tries to "fake" it, the problem is not that of performance, but of knowing what one is capable of and what one is not.

Successful leaders deal with that problem first. They do this first by knowing what their own competencies are, by accepting what they are capable of and what they are not capable of. They can fix that.

When they have achieved this kind of candor with themselves, they can see through others' pretenses. They can make candor about competence necessary and transparent.

For the most part, *people muddle through*, both in their work and in their private lives.

They excuse themselves for their incapacities. Then they seek out friends and acquaintances who will accept them and their deceits. They select friends and associates who will not challenge them. Competence not challenged on a daily basis will wither and decline.

Competent people thrive on challenges to their competence. Incompetent people will avoid challenges to their competencies if they can. And they will usually find a way to do so.

So most people, most of the time, will "muddle through" their work and private lives—if they can. It is a part of the leader's role to make this "muddling through" **impossible** in their organizations.

It is difficult to assess competence. That's because it is always relative. If you make it relative to the performance of others who are close by, you may be providing justification for mediocrity.

It *should* always *be* assessed against the *ideal*. Not that the ideal will ever be reached in full. But because that is the only practical fixed target there can be.

The "ideal" is not a destination. It is a way of life. People who are continuously learning how to perform better tomorrow than they did today are those who are actually *competent*. They are dedicated to their competence.

This requires that they make their organizations competent. No one can be fully competent in any organization which is not itself becoming more competent every day.

So assessing competence requires looking not at past performance or at credentials. It requires looking at how a person's—or an organization's performance is getting better . . . forever.

People who are competent have no choice but to get better. They are competent by habit, not by choice. And these habits of becoming more competent every day will drive them . . . forever.

Measuring or assessing competence cannot be revealed by looking at still shots. You have to look at the trajectory and the irreversible dedication to becoming more competence. It is the lust for more competence that characterizes competent people—and competent organizations.

Anything less than that is evidence of settling for the status quo—for the stultification that comes with self-satisfaction.

Competent people—and competent organizations—are *always* dissatisfied with past performance. It is a characteristic of competency. There is always the desire to do whatever it is they do better.

Without that compulsion, there is no way of becoming more competent. And without that perpetual **becoming**, there is no way to adequately assess the presence or absence of competence.

Keeping these preliminary observations in mind, we have a good platform for moving on to consider the many facets of individual competence.

There are many more of them than you may have imagined.

LEE THAYER

2. The Competent Individual

In this and the next two pieces in this book, we will explore in depth what constitutes individual competence. Actually, we will be exploring what *should* constitute individual competence in our thinking about it and therefore what we attempt to do about it.

We need to do this rather exhaustively as a precursor to talking intelligently about *organizational* competence.

That latter term is, of course, an example of "misplaced concreteness." Organization is an abstraction. Organizations cannot have directly the human attributes of competence. Only people and their interactions could be said to be competent—or not.

But we can use what we examine here as metaphors for what we want to examine when we get to organizations. The logic would remain the same. Organizations are more complex and it is more challenging to articulate the components of the organization, and to articulate the organization with its stakeholders and the larger world.

What we will do here and in the next two pieces is unpack the several facets of individual competence one at a time. When you think through these, keep in mind how you might translate into organizational competence.

The dictionary definition of competence is something like this:

> **Competence:** *the ability to do something successfully or consistently; (2) the scope of*

a person's or a group's knowledge or ability.

A person is **competent** if he or she has

> . . . *the necessary ability, knowledge or skill*
> *to do something successfully.*

Given the derivation of the term, it suggests that competency is merely *adequacy*.

That is not what we want to mean by it in this book. Here, we will want to mean something like

> *Being much more than barely adequate—*
> *moving in the direction of mastery if*
> *not virtuosity in the performance of one's role.*

In other words, we will want to avoid the commonly-held belief that "good enough" is good enough. It isn't.

For years, American auto manufacturers struggled with the notion of **quality**. To be competitive, they learned (albeit slowly) that "good enough" is not good enough when there is something available that is better.

So we have gone through several almost gimmicky schemes for being better than "good enough," from quality circles to total quality to six sigma, black belt, and beyond.

What we have learned is that quality is determined ultimately by customers and not by the latest and greatest in-house scheme.

So is every other aspect of a person's performance.

If we pay good money for a musical recital or a big stage performance, we expect far more than mere adequacy. We expect to have a wonderful *experience*—one that constitutes even a better-than-expected return on our investment.

This requires individual competence of a high order. If performance (in the eyes of the consumer) ranges from lousy to astounding, then what we want to mean by *competence* is near the upper end of that range.

This is how we want to conceive of and perceive *competence* in this book—not "adequate," but what drives a performance that meets or exceeds our expectations.

This is the understanding that underwrites the ensuing criteria for characterizing the **competent individual**.

A competent individual—

is one who is consciously and continuously **learning** how to perform his or her role(s) today **better** than yesterday.

Competence is not a destination. It is a way of life. Competent people are propelled always forward by a set of habits we might call "the learning mode." They are intensely curious about anything that might bear upon their performance, or their lives.

The competent person is always acutely dissatisfied with his or her past performance. They have a need or a lust to do everything they do today better than they did yesterday.

Those habits have people who are in the learning mode in their grasp. They don't *intend* to get better at what they do. They simply can't help it.

Mediocrity requires a bundle of habits developed over time. In the same way, competence requires a bundle of habits developed over time. The difference is that the competent individual *has to* get better. The mediocre person is self-satisfied, and satisfied with the status quo.

So a competent individual is one who is in motion—always compelled to critique past performance and to learn how to get better in his or her role(s).

Don't look for personality characteristics. The relevant characteristic is this inextinguishable yen to turn in a better performance tomorrow than today.

Obviously, this is not most people. People who are inescapably in the learning mode are rare. This does not imply that other people could not be in the learning mode. They were when they were children. Their parents, their teachers, their friends, the culture in general may have influenced them to believe that there are more important things than getting better and better—things like self-esteem and having "fun."

People will be in the learning mode if they have to. The SUFI writer Idries Shah says that the purpose of real learning is to enable learning more. We seem to have forgotten that in our culture and in our schools and homes.

We seem to want people to "find" themselves and their "bliss." There is no self to be "found." A person's self is a function of his or her competencies. One's bliss is therefore a function of how competent one is at performing his or her role(s) in life.

That is, of competence.

A competent person—

is one who is ready, willing, and *able* to *own* every problem that arises in the performance of his or her role(s) in life or at work.

Avoidance of responsibility is endemic in our culture. People don't want to *own* the problems they confront. They would usually prefer someone else to *own* those problems, so they can be "free to do their own thing."

People who do not have the ability to solve the problems they encounter often don't even see them. If those problems are disruptively personal, they will seek advice or help from anyone who might provide it.

We live in a welfare society. It is a mistake for the head of any organization to make of that organization a welfare organization. When the number of needy outweighs those who can carry them, the organization sinks.

To "own" the problem means roughly the competence to prevent it when possible, to take the lead in solving it when not. (But more on this key factor below.)

Owning creates a relationship. To "own" something means you are in a relationship with what you own. You belong to it, and it belongs to you.

A problem exists because someone says it exists. It exists in that person's interpretation of it. The person who perceives a problem is the one who names it. Whenever possible, it should be that person who "owns" it or champions its resolution.

The real issue here is that of capability: being *able* to own the problems that a person who—for strategic or logical reasons—*ought to* own.

It bears repeating here that a person who is not capable of solving a problem will either avoid perceiving it, or will slough it off for someone else to deal with.

Thus it is often a person's incompetence that stands in the way of accurately perceiving the surrounding world.

A competent person—

· is one who is also capable of ***anticipating*** the kinds of problems that will likely arise in the course of performing his or her role.

A competent surgeon does not enter OR without all of the support and resources that may be needed. Competent musicians carry with them an extra mouthpiece or bow, just in case. Competent plumbers arrive with the tools and other material they *might* need on a particular job. Competent CEOs have learned how to surround themselves with people whose capabilities complement their own.

Competent people have prepared for the problems that are likely to arrive. At the same time, they are especially alert to the symptoms of problems they may not have anticipated. So they are prepared for the unexpected.

Less than competent people often refer to such "surprises" as bad luck. They do not feel they are to be held responsible for anything that does not occur routinely.

To anticipate problems arising when you are attending to other problems is the order of the day for competent people. They are over-prepared.

Incompetent people are often under-prepared for even routine problems. Incompetent customer service people may get fifteen calls about the same problem. Yet they seem to be unprepared for the sixteenth call.

A competent person arrives at an interview prepared to take charge of it. Incompetent people are never prepared for this eventuality.

Hire the person who comes to interview *you*. If conducting the interview is totally your problem, you are facing an unlikely candidate.

It's not prescience. It is a matter of being prepared for whatever happens.

A competent individual—

is capable of ***precluding*** most of the problems that arise, and of ***obviating*** all of the other problems that do arise.

To *preclude* problems means designing yourself and your aims in life in such a way that the problems you do not want you will not have. Competent people do this by having specific aims and the kind of intelligence networks that alert them to potential problems along the way.

Anyone who tries to accomplish anything in this world will stir up problems. Most people avoid them by (a) having no particular aims in life, and (b) having networks of friends and entertainments that solidify their status quo. Being satisfied with who one is and with one's habits and beliefs will not preclude problems.

It will simply enable one not to feel responsible for them. If the government or an expert celebrity would just take care of them, one could continue to perform tomorrow much like today.

To *obviate* a problem means taking away the source(s) of its existence. Competent people obviate problems. They don't put a band-aid on them. They excise the *source* of the problem.

Merely "solving" problems usually leads to creating other problems. The solution creates the opportunity for other problems.

Problems must be eliminated not at the symptom level but at the level of the reasons for their existence.

This requires some astute forensic work. Most problems originate from incompetence. That may be the last thing an incompetent person would suspect. And thus the old saw:

> *Most people prefer a problem they can't solve to a solution they don't like.*

To undertake making oneself more competent strikes incompetent people as elitist and largely irrelevant. If they avoid a solution they don't like—or couldn't implement—someone or something else has to own the problem: a politician or a welfare program. Incompetent people believe they *deserve* to be bailed out. If they have been for years, it becomes a pattern that is difficult to break.

For example, in the typical school system, incompetent students—that it, those who can't or won't, whatever the reasons—account for as much as ten times more of the school's resources as do competent students.

They grow up expecting to be served by the larger society—not to serve it. Those who can and do—whatever their reasons—have to carry those who can't or won't. To aid those who can't is justifiable perhaps. But there is no welfare clerk who can distinguish those who *can't* from those who simply *won't*.

Add to this that years of being dependent on the larger society makes for habits that even *they* can't break.

> *As we will see, you can't make a competent organization out of incompetent people.*

Nor can incompetent people make a competent society, or even a competent relationship. If that's where many problems are bred, that condition has to be obviated.

A competent person—

requires no praise, punishment, or incentives for his or her performance.

She or he has developed the capacity to be their own best critics. Praise from people who perform better than they do might be appreciated. But not from those who are not competent.

Nor do they respond well to what is called "positive feedback." They know better than others how well they have performed and where they fell short.

Their rewards come from outperforming themselves, not from external incentives or rewards.

We live in a world that is largely ruled by incompetent people, since they outnumber competent people by far. In a voting democracy, they vote. They vote for what *they* want or need. They often actively dislike people who are more competent than they are.

It used to be known in Australia as "the tall poppy syndrome." Anyone who attempted to be a taller "poppy" than all the rest in the field would be shunned or undermined. There is some of that in the U.S. Youngsters in most schools who actually do their homework are called to task by negative labels. They have fewer "friends."

Where the power lies with the majority, and where the majority are at best mediocre, we have a limitless regression to the mean. So we pander to the incompetent. It is probably unintentional, but we unconsciously nurture a degree of incompetence in our society.

That's why we believe that positive feedback or self esteem will improve performance. It won't. But the mediocre performers call the shots.

> *We don't understand competent people. We have been too intent on understanding incompetent people.*

We therefore have a tendency to treat competent people the same way we have to treat incompetent people. This has the consequence of mistreating both.

A competent person—

has learned from experience that continuous growth in competence is its own reward.

No rewards from people who have shunned that experience is meaningful. Political correctness in our culture means that those who are superior performers should not criticize those who are inferior performers. But those who are inferior performers are subtly encouraged to criticize those who are more competent.

The women of Sparta believed it should be the other way around. Duty came first. If a son could not equip himself to do his duty, he was considered of little or no value.

We still expect that of our military and our firefighters. We still expect to be moved by the best performers when we pay to attend the theater.

A true leader shows that he *cares* about his or her people *by refusing to let them default themselves.* We are very elitest when it comes to selecting our own surgeons. But we do not seem to feel the same way about our children or the source of their influences.

Those who have not experienced the rewards of continuously expanding their competencies may believe that competence can be gained by a shortcut like rewards and incentives.

They would be simply wrong.

A competent person—

owns the problems of his or her performance, and thus *owns* the problems that arise on the path to his or her own destiny.

Incompetent people prefer to believe it is all a matter of luck or of the help to which they are "entitled." So they hope for the best from the world, not from themselves.

This demeans them, as they demean those who carry them on their backs.

"What do you want to be when you grow up?" That could be today, tomorrow, or ten years from now. The competent person *owns* the problem, and all of the challenges that go with it.

THE COMPETENT ORGANIZATION

Where competent people are concerned, the boss does not own the problems of their performance. *They* do.

They do not feel entitled. They feel responsible. The performance they agreed to, whether to themselves or to others, is the performance they will deliver. If they can't, they'll fix their shortfalls.

> **It is important to remember when you are contemplating all of these insights that there are no perfectly incompetent people. There are no perfectly competent people. Everyone at any point in time falls somewhere along the continuum. It is the more competent ones who strive to get better. The more incompetent ones look for salvation from some source outside of themselves.**

The (relatively) competent person—

seeks out challenges to their capabilities. They know that this is the best way to learn and grow.

The (relatively) incompetent person avoids such challenges. They are not in the learning mode, and hence avoid situations that might exceed their capabilities. They avoid learning whenever they can. They want to rely on what they already presume to know.

Competent people seek out people who are more competent than they are. They seek out situations in which they might even fail. They know that failure is often the best teacher. They do not rely on their past "experiences." They want to gain new ones in order to learn and grow.

The competent person has no fear of confronting an unfamiliar problem. Incompetent people stick to the problems they are familiar with.

> *If you're their boss, competent people will look to you as a special resource for their own growth—until you prove that you are not.*

3. The Competent Individual II

The competent individual—

is a question-asker, not an opinion-peddler.

Incompetent people are eager to synchronize what they know and how they feel with others around them. They tell people what they happen to know. They do not often consider what others may *need to* know. They do not know what they need to know, so they take what comes their way.

If they did know what they *need* to know, that would put them in the learning mode. And that condition is anathema to them.

Most people love sharing their opinions about things they know little about. The more their opinions overlap, the more likely they are to become friends, or to belong to the same network. They emulate one another.

They peddle their opinions to anyone who will listen. They like those who will listen. They don't like people whose opinions differ in significant ways.

There is a "catch" in all of this. If they like someone else, they will alter their opinions to fit. They are social chameleons until they belong to a group of people who have similar opinions. Then they stick together and become resistant to anything that might challenge their opinions.

A competent person, by contrast, is a question-asker. He or she is driven to grow and thus are forever asking questions that might challenge their own opinions.

They like people not because those people have similar opinions, but because they don't. They consider people who have a different take on things to be valuable. They are valuable because they expand one's own perspectives on things.

What questions?

Questions that are open-ended and lead somewhere, rather than confirm one's own predilections. Questions that put one's own perspectives at risk. Questions that get at the reality rather than ingrain the superficiality of most conversations.

It requires as much study and practice to become a superb question-asker as it does to become a concert pianist. It is the key characteristic of people who are in the learning mode. They even come to an interview with more and better questions than the interviewer has.

A good question is disruptive. It disrupts the chain of thought others might be caught up in. It disrupts their thinking, calls their operant mental models to task. It leads somewhere new rather than old. It forces learning and growth.

And how does a question-asker get to be masterful at it?

> *By practicing on himself or herself. They provoke their own learning and growth by calling their own opinions and assumptions into question. Then they are much better equipped to transform others into masterful question-askers.*
>
> *They ask, "What is the question you are answering?" when others persist in making statements.*
>
> *When disrobed, all facts are interpretations. This is what intrigues the question-asker.*
>
> *Because everything is based on human interpretations, the advantage always falls to those who see others' interpretations as the reality they have to deal with.*

The competent individual—

knows something that others are unlikely to know.

What the competent person knows that others don't is that competent people are happier, more in charge of their lives, and live longer. That's what the research shows.

Incompetent people don't believe this. Even if they are told, they reject it. In doing so, they are merely protecting their beliefs and their opinions.

They don't believe it because it requires experiencing it. It is not consistent with their experiences. It is consistent only with the experience that comes with becoming more competent.

Competent people know it because they have experienced it first-hand. Competent people are open to experiences that are outside of the conventional. Incompetent people are not.

It is the case that competent people are always dissatisfied with their past *performance*. But this is not about them. It is about their performance, which can be improved upon continuously . . . forever. Incompetent people take it personally. They do not separate their feelings about their performance from feelings about themselves.

Incompetent people assume they have to remodel themselves when someone critiques their performance. This is hard to accept and even harder to implement. Competent people assume that the critique (which comes primarily from themselves) is not about who they are but about their performance, which can be much more readily improved upon.

Competent people are happier because they are always learning and growing. And growth = life.

The unhappiest people are those who believe that their lives are being controlled by fate, or by others. This is somewhat paradoxical, because people who are merely living out what fate handed them often report being happier because it would be hopeless to strive or to aspire.

So perhaps the better term is simply having more life. Competent people seem to have more life in them than do others. Becoming more competent generates more life.

THE COMPETENT ORGANIZATION

Certainly competent people believe they have more control over their lives. They have demonstrated it to themselves.

That they collectively live longer is a function of always having something more to achieve. They have a future. Incompetent people don't look forward to a future that recycles the past.

*Incompetent people **hope**. Competent people **do**.*

It's a difference that makes a difference.

The competent person—

lives by this premise:

Learning = growth, and growth = life.

They have experienced it. They have studied competent people's lives. They have read the research. Those are the conclusions.

Being in the learning mode does not mean adding to what you already know. It means having what you were certain of displaced by a better understanding. This requires questioning what you already know.

Physical growth has finite limits. Not so the life of the mind. That growth of the mind, of the *self*, can be advantageously pursued right up to the final curtain.

The learning mode is not something one can opt into or out of by willing it. The learning mode is a bundle of habits developed over years of learning. The main thing you gain from learning is the capacity for more—and better—learning. You can never know, or do, everything.

The mind grows slowly the more garbage it has to shuffle around. Learning something of value requires unlearning its predecessor. The learner seeks better and more pertinent perspectives. There is always a trade-off.

The proposition that growth = life is so well documented that there is no question. Who exhibits the most life? Young children, who are irrepressibly into learning everything that eludes them.

Who has the least real life? Those who presume to know everything they need to know to survive socially.

Learning involves risk. And, as we know, risk stimulates being totally alive.

The competent person—

is one who **knows what he or she *needs* to know—and acquires it.**

This runs directly contrary to our notion of "education" in the Western world.

Competent people develop their own communication networks—*inductively.* Less competent people are more passive. They take what comes. Their communication networks are *deductive.* That is, what they input is decided by someone else. That someone else may be a friend or acquaintance, a boss, a teacher, or the media.

This is a key factor for competent organizations, as we will see. Here, we need to note only what kinds of difference this makes.

People who do not have clear goals or aims in life have no solid way of determining what they need to know. Those who have a purpose in life can be constantly aware of what they need to know.

The conventional Western educational system is based on such premises as these:

- Students or children as such don't know what they need to know. So a teacher or an educational hierarchy needs to decide for them what they need to know. Those "experts" or elected officials develop the knowledge machinery directed at students deductively.

- Even if the students have an inkling of what they need to know, the premise is that they wouldn't be able to find it. So not only the content of education but the methods as well are determined by people often unknown to the students.

- Parents and teachers (as well as preachers) usually operate on the same premises.

- Learning is not about learning *how* but about learning *what*. Tests as typically tests of what has been memorized. There are few tests that measure the ability to seek out and acquire what one needs to know.

- What's important in this kind of system is not what you *need* to know, but what you happen to know.

- So there is always an "expert" of some sort who functions between those who have a need to know and a body of knowledge presumed to address that need. Again, this is based in deductive thinking.

It isn't that deductive systems are wrong. They significantly take away from the person(s) involved the *need* to learn what they need to know, and how to go about *acquiring* it.

Thus we have the larger mass of people in our society who are incompetent at both—**both deciding what they need to know, and learning how to acquire it.**

Unintentionally, we nurture incompetence, not competence. It is expected that competent people will simply have to swim upstream.

Much of society (like our educational system) is built to accommodate incompetent people. The assumption is that competent people should fend for themselves against alien systems.

The competent person—

strives to provide others around him or her with what those *others* need to know, when and where they need it. The competent person is thinking inductively in a deductively-created social system.

That kind of thinking conflicts with the system built to provide whatever it provides on the assumption that this is what people should have. Competent people are both disliked and often punished or undercut for their way of thinking.

A critical mass of competent people will attract and retain competent people. They like to be around each other, in the same way that incompetent people like to be around each other.

If you have a critical mass of marginally-competent people, they will have the most influence on the culture of your organization. Offloading the incompetent people and replacing them with competent people requires time, patience, and ingenuity.

It is the one thing that leaders of conventional organizations fail at most often. They underestimate the power of the majority, and underestimate what has to be done to achieve this shift from incompetence to competence. Individuals often cannot make this transition themselves because of the capabilities and commitment involved.

The competent person attempts to know at all times where the power lies, and how to work with it or achieve in spite of it. If they don't have it, they know that they need to be supported by those who do.

The competent individual—

both **demands** and **nurtures** competence in all others with whom he or she must deal at work—and sometimes in daily encounters outside of work!

Particularly within their own sphere, competent people are extremely discriminating. It's a judgment they often can't hide. They know competence when they encounter it. And they are pained by incompetence when they encounter *that*.

They expect the people they interact with to be as competent as they are. If they are not, competent people are quick to help them become more competent. They know that competence is not an inborn trait. It must be, and can be learned.

Competent people are demanding of others. But they are also generous as teachers or mentors. If another wants or needs help, the competent person will provide it.

Sympathetically but with great finesse, the competent person exhibits how much he or she *cares about* other people by refusing to let them default themselves.

The competent person—

thus makes a great team player. First of all, he or she understands that it is not about them. It is about the performance of the team or the ensemble.

Competent people understand that when it is time to solo, they have to be over-prepared. When it is another person's time to solo, the competent person provides world-class support for that person's performance.

The best music (and military and sports) ensemble is comprised of people who are clearly great performers and getting better with every performance. But they are also proficient in the role of enhancing the performance of others when their turn comes.

Organizations, as we will see, should be composed this way—made up of virtuoso ensembles that make the whole organization perform better.

Max DePree was the past Chairman and CEO of Herman Miller, Inc., and gathered many accolades for his organization. This was the idea behind his book *Leadership Jazz.* It was about how competent people make everybody else look better.

The competent individual—

is not ambitious in the sense of wanting to "climb the ladder" to the top. The competent person merely wants to be the best there ever was in his or her present role and endeavors.

The competent person is not status-conscious, but performance conscious. If status or celebrity comes his way, he is grown up enough to be humble about all the deference. He or she is quick to give credit to all of the others who contributed to their performance.

The competent person is too busy getting better in his or her role to pay much attention to the politics that pollute the environment in which they make their way. If you want to get better tomorrow than you were today, you don't have time to play games, to compete for the limelight.

The competent person is willing to let his or her performance speak for itself.

If he or she stumbles, they are quick to take the credit and use it to learn from. If success occurs, the competent person quickly gives others the credit they deserve.

No one in any ensemble—including any organization—was ever successful by themselves. Their success *always* required supporting roles. Their success, if it comes, is *always* supported by the competence of those in supporting roles.

People who don't understand this are not really competent people. They are deluded people who do not understand what it takes to perform competently. They are in it not to improve their performance, but to enhance their status.

Such people, no matter how "successful" they might be seen to be by their fans, are not really competent people. They are self-serving people who could never do an ensemble or an organization any good.

In an ensemble, they would be constantly competing for the spotlight. In an organization, they would depend upon politicking their way to the top.

*It makes a great difference **why** people want to be seen as competent.*

The competent person—

understands that the only authentic way to love life—**and to be loved by life in return**—is to become really, really good at whatever they choose to do.

People love their work only if they are good at it. To assume that the path to the good life is to find something to do that you love is wrongheaded. You can't love something you can't do well.

THE COMPETENT ORGANIZATION

Incompetence generates deficient love, mere play-acting. It is competence that produces real love.

It is only truly competent people who understand that. People who are incompetent may profess love. But only those who are competent at delivering it can provide the real experience.

Competent people are always learning. They know that it is learning that engenders life. "Knowing" diminishes life unto death.

It may be difficult or impossible to convince people of this. They have to experience it to understand it. That's why learning to be more and more competent requires the internal and/or external *necessity* to do so at the outset.

This may even sound counter-intuitive. Why should it have to be made *necessary* for people to gain a richer life? It will either be made necessary for themselves as individuals out of their own consciences and habits. Or it will have to be made necessary by those who mentor or parent them. It's what leaders do.

Competent people *care* about themselves. That's why they refuse to default themselves.

Incompetent people care little about themselves and less about other people. That's why it is easy for them to default themselves and all others they have contact with.

There has to be sufficient necessity to drive continuous learning and growth. What is not internal has to be provided externally. If the combination is not sufficient, learning—and growth—will not continue to occur.

The aim is always to internalize or inculcate the habits and perspectives that provide the sufficient necessity.

To be continued . . .

4.   The Competent Individual III

The competent individual—

cannot be "cloned." Competent people are each unique, one-of-a-kind, non-standard.

It is incompetent people who can be cloned. They are more or less substitutable for one another. They can even be replicated by technological devices like automation. A robot is simply an incompetent person.

Competent people cannot at present be replaced by robots. The robots have to be standardized, which is a characteristic of incompetent people.

It may be possible to create robots that learn and grow in competency.

But they will never overtake the most competent people (who are not the fans of "Jeopardy"). There is no way to program the creative improvising that is the hallmark of competent people.

Competent people grow in life. Robots grow out of more clever programming. If the scientizers succeed in reducing life to programming, then indeed the robots will be running the place. Incompetent people will be the first to become redundant.

We will still need competent people to program the next generation of robots.

In the meantime, McDonald's will continue to run on automated programs in the kitchen. The order-taker will become automated. But not the customers. They *cannot be* reduced to a computer program.

And when there is no longer the need for humans to make the process problematic, what would the point of that be?

We seem to disdain real competence in our culture. We will replace it if we can.

Who would want to live in a world in which everything—and everyone—is pre-programmed? Apparently, the incompetents of the world would.

After all, *they* seem to be programmed to be liked by others just like them, and to be essentially irrelevant to anything beyond them.

Perfect, for those who want to live amongst drones and clones.

The competent person—

is fundamentally and by habit an ROA person.

ROA stands for Return on Attention. Competent people know that this is their key strategic tool. The most precious thing they have to invest is their attention. If they don't get a good return from their attention, they know they can neither learn nor grow.

They attend to certain people who are worth attending to—whether directly or indirectly. Since the one person they must attend to whether they choose to or not is themselves, they make their inner voice always worth paying attention to.

They acquire certain input to their thinking from the smartest people they can find. Not the fastest or the most acclaimed. That might be an ancient philosopher or a current thinker in any field.

They don't offer advice to those who can't or won't pay attention. Even then, only if asked.

This enables the competent person to be thoroughly *engaged* in his or her work and role. They know that lack of engagement is a way of wasting time.

They have a purpose for every encounter with their own minds or with other minds. They don't have conversations. They pursue goals.

They are not collectors of trivia. They are actively after what is useful to them given their aims in life.

They are consciously frugal in what they listen to and what they say. To competent people, less is more.

They are not trying to be "perfect." They are just devoting their precious attention to matters that enable them to get better at what they do.

They develop the habits that keep them focused, no matter what is going on. To a competent person, reading a good book vs. watching a bad movie (or even the heavily-edited-for-dramatic-effect news) is a choice. Their aims in life make the choice for them.

They are always "up to something." Like Patton, they do not talk about what they are up to.

Competent people do not talk on and on about what they are going to do. They just do it.

The competent individual—

knows that he or she is always performing *some* role, and that they will be judged by others not according to who they are or by their intentions, but by their *performance*.

As Yoda (in *Star Wars*) said: "There is no **try**. There is only **do**."

Competent people do not try "to the best of their ability"—whatever that might mean. For them, any time is "show-time." They are being watched and judged.

THE COMPETENT ORGANIZATION

They perform to the consequences, not to the script. They have to be so competent that they can improvise on the spot. They are pursuing the desired consequences, not looking for approbation.

They do not try to please. They perform the role required to achieve the consequences needed.

They would agree with Shakespeare, who said (paraphrased) that

> *All the world's a stage, and*
> *We are but players on it.*

Our roles and how we play them carries us to our destinies. The better we play them, the better the outcomes.

One useful way of thinking about this is that you are always playing a role. You are auditioning before yourself or before others to be acknowledged in that role. It is your expectations—and theirs—that legitimate who you *are*.

It is who you *are* because they cannot see *you*. All they can see is your performance. In this pop-psych world of ours, you can get down on yourself or misread your performance.

You can make it personal. You may take others' reactions personally. But all they have to go on is your performance.

You are always auditioning. Audition for the role you need.

That is the only path you can have.

Competent people are always auditioning as competent people. To be judged as competent, you have to perform competently.

The competent individual—

is obsessive about his or her commitments—whether those are commitments to others, or to themselves.

Not distressingly so. Competent people always develop their capabilities to meet or exceed their obsessions. Incompetent people may take a pill. But competent people view their commitments as problems to be solved, and set about solving them.

Another way of seeing this is that, for competent people, excuses are anathema. They never get good at offering excuses in lieu of achieving what they promise. That's because they don't practice making excuses like incompetent people do.

Can people become "competent" at making excuses? Not really. If incompetent people surround themselves with those who will accept excuses in lieu of accomplishment, it may look like competence. But it is merely the incompetent endorsing the incompetent.

Competence means competence in the pursuit of worthy goals.

In an adversarial relationship (think master criminals vs. master detectives like Sherlock Holmes) the more competent person always has the advantage in the long run.

But in a complex "democratic" society such as our own, it isn't the competent people who have the advantage but the incompetent people. They have more votes. They must be "protected" which has come to mean pandered to by government policy.

We don't often elect competent people for key roles because that is decided by people who often are not themselves competent. They dislike any form of competence that offends them. And they have the numbers to do something about it.

So it would be unrealistic to assume that competent people have the long range advantage in our society.

Nonetheless: given the advantage to people who do strive to improve their performance regularly, parents and teachers and CEOs have the unique opportunity to demand increasing competence on the part of their own children, their own students, or their own associates.

The more competence that can be developed in our society, the better off everyone would be. And the better the prognosis for our society.

The competent individual—

wants to be tested and challenged. The incompetent person wants to be protected. He or she prefers the security of anonymity, while still claiming to deserve the best life has to offer.

These are two very different mindsets.

The competent person seeks out what may be more challenging than what he or she has already been exposed to. The incompetent person prefers no change, prefers a familiar routine, and avoids anything that challenges his or her thinking.

The competent person seems to follow a suggestion from Eleanor Roosevelt— that you should always do what you don't know how to do. This stretches you. This is the path of growth.

The competent person reads not for confirmation of his or her present thinking, but for challenges to it. The competent person wants to learn about what he or she does not already know. Peter Drucker, for example, chose every year an area of knowledge he knew nothing about. He spent the year studying it.

The more incompetent you are in your role, the more likely it is that you will follow others and choose to read the best-sellers in your field.

Competent people risk learning and thus changing. Incompetent people abhor personal change.

The competent individual—

is the one who is more creative, more inventive, more capable of improvising when the recipe fails.

Those who are less than fully competent are far more likely to *emulate* not the best, but those who happen to have status in their local networks. They do not emulate the most competent. They have little cognizance of them, and can't discern the competent from the incompetent.

They do not expose themselves to ideas that are not commonplace. They prefer to let their "friends" do that for them. They are fans of those who their friends are fans of.

Being creative requires a level of discipline that only competent people achieve. Michelangelo once said: *"Creativity is a function of discipline."* It is not a function of the absence of constraints. It is a function of the kind of constraints imposed on oneself by competence.

The more you know, the more you *can* know. The more you learn, the more you *can* learn.

Part of competence is the capacity to break free of the restrictions of an existing mental model. Finding a better way is a trademark of the competent person.

It seems to me that this is what Michelangelo was getting at.

Creativity comes on top of competence at a task or in a role—not in lieu of it.

Competent people know that there are many paths to an accomplishment, including the necessity of inventing one when the path is blocked or otherwise not feasible.

Improvising under duress is the competent person's forte. It is a way of crashing through boundaries. It is a way of giving expression to one's feelings, aims in life. It is a way of moving toward one's goals when there is no other path to take.

This has to be a part of who the competent person *is*. Proficiency at improvising cannot be simply willed. It has to be learned and made a part of who one is over time.

Competence is a many-faceted condition of mind, of spirit, and of heart.

It enables passion to become functional.

What people can't, they won't.

*When people **can**, they might.*

> *Having a vision is one thing. Being able to fulfill it requires extreme competence.*

The competent individual—

bets on himself. Less competent people are more likely to bet on things outside themselves.

Competent people unconventionally put themselves at risk. They know that there is no great achievement without comparable risk.

In putting themselves out there to test themselves, competent people have more drama in their lives. Not only does this give them more life, but it provides immunity to the pap drama that pours out of the media.

Vicarious drama is safe. But it adds nothing to a person's stature—or to his or her character—or to his or her capacity for creating their own.

Playing a subordinate role in someone else's drama is not appealing to competent people. Not, that is, unless that other person has a better story to tell than even they have.

Incompetent people are consumers. Competent people are producers. Incompetent people have settled for being-done-to. Competent people are doers.

The competent person—

focuses on the accomplishment, while others focus on themselves.

Competent people are capable of "de-centering"—that is, of getting outside of themselves to perceive and pursue their aims in life. Their aims are more important than are their personal feelings or interests at the moment.

Incompetent people rarely exhibit that capability.

Competent people live for their accomplishments. Incompetent people want accomplishments handed to them. In doing so, incompetent people lose what's important about life. In doing so, competent people gain what is really important in life—growing in their abilities to pursue meaningful goals in life.

The competent individual—

is capable of performing **triage** in the midst of the happenings of the moment—and in the midst of a trajectory gone wrong.

What this means is that the competent person can discriminate what is pertinent to him or her at the moment and what is not. What this means is that when you know precisely what the consequences have to be (no matter how incriminating or illogical the process of getting there may seem), you can figure out in a flash what comes first, what next, and so on.

In one sense, then, competent people are always engaged in performing *triage* on their own lives. Once it is a habit, it requires no special effort. It requires no more effort to perform triage than to be a coach potato, once the habits are ingrained.

It all hinges on these three:

- Having specific criteria for what comes first, second, etc.;
- Subordinating yourself to that course of thought and action; and
- Harboring the competencies that enable you to act accordingly.

The competent individual—

is self-empowered. The power comes from his or her competence.

It is not power over other people. It is power over oneself. To be highly disciplined provides its own power—both of action and of attraction.

The competent person is also *relevant*. He or she is relevant to a worthy cause which is greater than they are. This kind of relevance provides status. It provides status in one's own eyes, which is the best and most resilient status there is.

It is one thing to be "liked." It is quite another to be respected for what one is capable of.

It may be that the only respect a competent person earns is from other competent people. But that is the only kind of respect that matters in the long run. Incompetent people depend upon mutual captivation. This keeps them at status quo.

Competent people want to be pushed and pulled into a higher level of competence. Incompetent people react to this as an intrusion on their prerogative to choose irrelevance.

Relevance for the right reasons enhances life. Irrelevance impoverishes life. It is the right choice that empowers.

The competent person—

is rarely if ever adversarial. Knowing that incompetent people take him or her to be an adversary, the competent person feels responsible to teach the incompetent person how to be more competent. If successful, this releases the incompetent person from his or her bondage.

Competent people are teachers and mentors—never parading superiority. They do not want to be anyone's better. They want to better themselves. They want this for their own quality of life, not to feel superior to anyone else.

The riches in their way of life they want to share with others. They know that they cannot confer a benefit on an unwilling person (an ancient bit of Greek wisdom). They must do this out of their hearts, not their minds.

Competent people function like stewards of a way of life that others could achieve if they are willing.

Beyond that, competent people do not interfere.

If they care, they will refuse to let that other person default himself or herself. Not because they feel superior. But because they are familiar with a way of life that is better—better for the best of us or for the worst of us.

They sing the praises of a life well lived, not of themselves.

Incompetent people—

Have the problem of "killing" time—especially at work.

Competent people have the problem of prioritizing how to *invest* their time for the best all-around return.

PART II

In Part I, we examined in depth the concept of individual competence. We needed to do that in order to have the right platform to stand on to explore in this part of the book what constitutes the competence of *organizations*.

The criteria remain the same. So we can safely but thoughtfully use all of the preceding as analogies for launching into our examination of the competence of *organizations*.

For example, if we pay money for the performance of the people on stage in the theater, we expect competence. We also expect competence on the part of the writer, the director, the stage manager, the acoustic designer of the theater itself, and so on.

If we pay money for the product or the services of an organization, we expect competence. We pay good tax money for the government agencies we have to deal with. But we don't always get either competence or a pleasant experience. Why is that?

In the following pages, we will examine what competence means to the users of an organization. We will explore the sources of its competence or incompetence. We will thus be laying the foundation for moving on to how competent organizations need to be composed and how and why they must of necessity function differently.

In Rama Jager's book *In the Company of Giants*, the founder and head of Cypress Semiconductor T. J. Rogers is quoted as saying:

There are no safe harbors—the only safe harbor is competency.

We can take that as a splendidly succinct way of thinking about what we are about to explore. Keep it in mind.

*We too often **assume** the requisite competence.*
We ought not. It is the most critical factor.

5. The Competent Organization: I

What could the CEO of Cypress Semiconductor have meant (previous page) when he said that "the only safe harbor is competency"?

It's a appealing metaphor. But do competent people or competent organizations *seek* a safe harbor? You might well imagine that it would be the *incompetent* organization that seeks a "safe harbor."

Doesn't a competent person or organization seek to be tested against whatever might come? Isn't it incompetence that seeks an untroubled existence where the status quo could grow?

There is something about the word "safe" that is troubling.

Competent people are always in the learning mode. And learning = growth, not guaranteed to be "safe." "Safe" occurs only when there is little or no change.

Competency is not a safe harbor. It is a journey. It is the never-ending pursuit of *better*.

There are no still waters in that journey. There are always agitated waters—the agitation being provided by the pursuit of getting better. That requires learning. And the best learning always produces growth. There is nothing placid about growth.

So probably what Rodgers meant by his metaphor is that the only path to survival and success is competency. Let's go with that.

Given our insights and revelations about the competent individual, we have a good place to stand to explore what we ought to mean by a competent *organization*.

A competent organization—

is one that provides its users with the overall feelings of a good experience that comes from having their expectations met or exceeded.

Feelings? Yes. All interactions a person has with the world have as their first component emotions. An expectation met or failed produces feelings, one way or the other. A dinner out is first an emotional thing. We either had a great experience, a humdrum experience, or a bad experience.

We may translate that experience into words. But they would be words about our feelings. Marketers are only now beginning to realize that it is their *experience* that customers and other users are after. It is not the product or the service as such. They may talk about the tangibles. But it is the intangibles—even the unsaid—that constitute their underlying expectations.

It is the positive or negative feelings engendered by the whole process that comprise the experience.

The airlines know better than ever how to get their aircraft from Point A to Point B. But they have forgotten how to make it the kind of special experience it used to be. And "customer service" has grown to gargantuan size and shape in direct proportion to the lack of customer service.

The automated voice may ask you if you want to talk in English or Swahili. But it doesn't ask you why you are on the phone in the first place.

Various technologies have come to replace the process of providing the right experience. If an organization is overwhelmed with calls about a user's problems, is the answer to put a band-aid on it just because the organization has that capability?

Maybe precluding the problems that users are calling about would be more effective and even more economical?

Users, then. Different users comprise different constituencies.

Every organization is supported by its users in one way or another. The employees use the organization for their own purposes. They will unless there is enlightened leadership that makes all of the members of a given organization into stewards of the organization's mission in life. The lessons provided by Admiral Lord Nelson's leadership show how this can be done.

Organizations have customers or clients. Some government agencies are supposed to serve citizens with respect to what the government requires of its citizens. They are users.

Investors attempt to make money via their financial arrangements with organizations. They are users.

Local, state, and federal tax collectors are users. Consultants and advisors would be bereft without organizations they can use for their purposes. Suppliers are users, even though the organization may be using its suppliers.

The local and national economies have a stake in the organizations that make it flourish or flounder. They are thus nameless "stakeholders."

Civilizations depend upon their organizations for their own destiny. They thus have a vested interest in the health and welfare of their organizations.

And so on. Organizations are intertwined with all of their constituencies. And vice versa.

Their constituencies, on which they depend for their existence, all have a vested interest in the organization.

How well the organization serves those constituencies determines in large part the life and the destiny of that organization.

How *competent* the organization is in serving the best self-interests of those constituencies determines the health and the welfare of that organization.

This is no incidental matter. It **is** what matters.

The competent organization—

is, like the competent individual, one that is, unlike the competent individual, continuously learning to get better at *everything* it does.

As emphasized previously, this is an example of "misplaced concreteness." *Organization* is an abstraction. Abstractions are not capable of learning—only people are. Organizations *can* perform better. This requires not only improvement in the performance of every role in the organization, but better systems and processes, and pushes and pulls in the culture of the organization that underwrite the necessity for continuously getting better.

People who are irreversibly in the *learning mode* generally make the best members of any group, ensemble, team, or organization.

It's likely you do not hire for that characteristic. You are more likely to look at credentials and/or previous experience. Those may or may not be of value. What is of greater value is that people who are in the learning mode will sooner or later overtake the performance of others who may initially be more "talented" or have more pertinent experience.

That's one advantage. Another is that experienced people look at the world as if through a microscope. They fit their interpretations of what is going on to the theories they bring to their perceptions.

People in the learning mode see the world as if through a telescope. They are constantly looking more broadly, and deeper, for anything that might bear on their performance in their roles. They want to learn how to do what they do better. They don't start with a "success paradigm" like those having more "experience" do. They start with a need to learn—to get better, to grow.

So people in the learning mode are always better candidates in the long run. They may not know how. But they will learn how—quickly. They do not cling to past theories or mental models, but always seek to find better ones.

A "learning organization" is one filled with people who are in the learning mode. For those who are not, it must become a necessity—either directly, or indirectly via an organizational culture that makes it both **possible**, and **necessary**.

The operable term here is BETTER. There must be a sense of urgency about performing better today than yesterday.

If the newcomer does not arrive with that internal sense of urgency, it must be provided externally—by leaders and by mentors.

When a clear majority of the people who comprise the organization are in the learning mode, the culture will be biased in that direction. In a conventional organization, it is the high performers who are made to feel uncomfortable by the organization's culture. In a high-performance organization (the ideal to navigate by), it is the underperformers who will feel uncomfortable. They usually leave of their own volition.

If it is not necessary to get better and better, it will not happen. This necessity may be internal. But if it is not, it must be provided externally by the way the organization is composed—and then ideally by a culture that makes better performance both possible, and **necessary**.

A competent organization—

is one that is ready, willing, and able to field successfully every problem or obstacle or opportunity that comes its way. To be that kind of organization, it must be prepared and equipped to deal effectively with the *unexpected*.

Conventionally, we have had the notion that a competent person is one who can handle satisfactorily whatever is *expected*. But in looking at it the way we do in this book, it is clear that competence is more than that. It requires the capabilities and the preparedness to deal effectively with the *unexpected*.

It is advantageous to take the same stance with respect to the competent organization.

What this requires is as follows:

- Thoroughly competent people in every key role in the organization;
- Habits and systems of surveillance that reveal potential problems or opportunities at the time they just begin to emerge; and

- The organizational flexibility that enables the person who identifies and thus **owns** the problem to recruit anyone deemed useful in solving the problem.

What this in turn implies is:

- That competent people by definition want to test themselves against problems that arise—the tougher the better.
- That competent people know in advance the contributions that others—inside or outside the organization—are equipped to provide.
- That those competent people are capable of deflecting or isolating the problem while they resolve it.
- That the person who **owns** the problem knows to whom and how to report the problem and the solution that solved it, or is underway.

As we saw earlier, competent people are capable of identifying the hidden cause(s) of the problem, and therefore of obviating it—that is, doing what needs to be done to preclude the same problem from occurring again in the future.

Most organizations are guilty of spending too much time, with too many incompetent or irrelevant people, in meetings about problems.

Incompetent people love to see the same problem recur again because they now have an answer they don't have to think about.

Competent people don't want to see the same problem again. They want to hone themselves on the unexpected.

The lesson is this: Don't talk about "the" problem. Talk only about *whose* problem.

You want the person or persons closest to the problem—the ones who have identified it—to own it, from identifying and precluding it, or solving and obviating it.

There may be an occasional problem that requires organization-wide attention. That requires the leader and his or her team. But the more local you can keep problems, and **IF** you have competent people, the better and more efficiently they will be dealt with.

It will always, in the end, come back to how competent the people in key roles are.

This applies equally to opportunities. Let the person who identifies it own it. You want people to be competently entrepreneurial about both problems and opportunities.

Never take over ownership of problems if—

- *Someone closer to it **should** own it.*
- *The organization is composed in such a way that the most competent people own the most relevant problems and/or opportunities.*

As leader, your first task is to compose the organization so that you are dispensable. You are NOT the most competent person to take over every problem that happens to appeal to you.

If you are the greedy, egotistical CEO who loves to show off and take ownership of the problems *you* like to deal with, you will never have a competent organization.

The competent organization—

is one that is capable of *anticipating* the problems (or opportunities) it will encounter along the path it is on.

This requires being on the right path. If you are on the wrong path, you will invest your life dealing with problems that are irrelevant to your cause. The test of being on the right path is that you face the problems that would necessarily occur on *that* path.

It is far easier to deal with a problem that is just emerging than one that is full-blown.

This requires three kinds of competencies:

- The kind of imagination that comes only from being fully competent;

- The kind of competence that enables seeing what is different about problems encountered—not what is the same; and

- The competence required to solve the problem encountered, for it will otherwise not be seen, or will be avoided.

Competent people—and therefore competent organizations—have both a different mentality and very different and more proactive imaginations. They have the kind of imagination that reaches deeper into possibilities rather than merely constraints.

Most people try to identify problems by looking for how similar they are to a previous problem. Competent people—and thus competent organizations—do not. They look for dissimilarities. Or they imagine that the problem is one they have not encountered before. It is approached as if it were new. There are always advantages in doing it this way.

Finally, people have a selective blindness to problems they can't imagine being able to solve.

The more competent people are, the more likely they are to anticipate problems, and the more likely their characterization of the problem will be correct.

A competent organization—

does not praise people for accomplishing what is called for in those people's role descriptions. They are merely doing what they agreed to do.

Competent organizations do not reward people for meeting the expectations they agreed to, any more than they expect praise for merely meeting their customers' or their stakeholders' expectations.

It's when those expectations are enthusiastically and uniquely *exceeded* that there might be considerations of praise.

Nor do competent organizations punish people for not accomplishing what they had agreed to accomplish. There *may* be extenuating circumstances.

But this is not the key factor. The key factor is that competent people have critical consciences. They know when they have performed well. They know when they have performed poorly. If people don't have this level of conscientiousness, you would not want them in your—competent—organization.

Competent people are reluctant either to reward or punish themselves. The value of the experience lies in the value of what they taught themselves as a result of the experience.

The conscience of an organization is at the heart of its culture. If you have a critical mass of competent people, they will do no wrong. They will do the right thing. If it turns out well—or badly—they will learn how to perform better next time.

Incentives always backfire. Neither provide them to your users nor expect any from them. It's the reality that counts in the long run, not any tricks along the way.

The competent organization—

is not the one that is growing in size or capitalization. It is the one that is growing in competence.

An organization can be likened to a ship. Its financial performance is represented by its wake. But there is nothing in that wake that tells it whether or not it is going in the right direction.

The only growth that is reliably worth measuring is growth in competence. Because that leads to more competence. A competent ship may not make the biggest wake. But it makes the best wake. That's because it is moving in the right direction, gaining in performance as it goes.

Growth in both the mind's reach and its grasp can be continuous. That kind of growth depends upon intentional habits. That necessity can be built into organizations.

"Reach" refers to the breadth and depth of one's mental habits. "Grasp" refers to increasingly competent interpretations of what is going on—the sheer ability to comprehend more, and to comprehend better.

What doesn't grow stagnates. Like stagnant waters, it becomes poisonous. Where the mind is concerned, it poisons its owner's reach *and* grasp, and eventually leads to shrinking into oblivion.

In organizations, what is required is disruption—disruption of habits of thought and of action. It is the organization's leaders who must disrupt the routines of the status quo. Those routines may have served well enough in the past. But any organization that is not growing "mentally" will minimally be out of touch with an ever-changing world.

All organizations are potentially subject to a condition much like Alzheimer's. The more irrelevant the mind is in the scheme of things, the more it is subject to ossification.

Organizations ossify around ways of thinking and of doing that are no longer relevant to a changed and changing world. They die by status quo.

That's why the remarkable past-CEO of ABB, Percy Barnevik, considered the status quo to be the enemy—needing to be snuffed out wherever it was taking root.

When it is just sprouting, it is extinguishable with the proper extinguisher—the disruptive leader. When it is full grown, as in an ossified bureaucracy, it is far more difficult—sometimes impossible—to kill.

Where there is not growth in competence in organizations, there is something growing akin to inoperable cancer. The only way to deal with it effectively is to preclude it.

The competent organization—

embraces the problem it encounters on its chosen path toward its aims in life.

It has a culture that is hungry for bigger and more challenging problems and obstacles. That's because these are seen as the sources of provocation for learning and for growth.

Growth in competence is a way of life. Problems and obstacles are not onerous things that get in the way. They are the source of the energy that comes from the appetite for growth in competence.

The competent organization—

is a collective where people have *fun*.

Not the kind of fun most people think of as "fun"—which is an escape from life. But the kind of fun that competent people who are engaged in a life of becoming more competent enjoy.

Competence generates its own rewards. A truly competent performer is having fun. The fun comes from being so good at what he or she does that they can *play* at doing what they do.

When competent people perform in an ensemble—or an organization—they excite and turn each other on by their competent performances and improvisations. They are fully engaged in what they do as a result of being fully competent at doing it. There is a friendly competition at getting better, of surprising others at how much better they can get.

Competent people raise the performance of one another. Incompetent people diminish or inhibit the performance of others.

A competent organization performs like a competent individual, always getting better at what they choose to do. In addition, a competent organization is always striving to get better not in one or two ways, but at *everything* it does.

To be continued . . .

"In a hierarchy, each employee tends to rise to his level of incompetence; the cream rises until it sours."
—The Peter Principle (1969)

6. The Competent Organization: II

When Laurence J. Peter published his book in 1969, it was taken as humorous satire.

But there was always some kernel of elusive truth—at least of reality—in most of his commentaries. He was much copied. As has been said, that is a sincere form of flattery.

But consider it more carefully. The hidden reality is something like this:

> When people are promoted in a hierarchy, they move into a role which they have usually not been in. They are therefore not competent (as yet) in that role. If they do succeed in that new role, they become candidates for a next-higher role.
> In his much-repeated but rarely heeded maxim, the process is laid bare. If you are the "cream," you will likely be promoted. You will be promoted until you arrive in a role in which you are stuck by your own incompetence—which you are incapable of mastering. Thus "the cream rises until it sours."

This is more or less commonplace in conventional organizations. The best get promoted until they arrive at a higher role they are incapable of learning how to perform competently.

From birth until death people fall into (or choose into) roles they have never been in before. We have to *learn* how to perform in those roles. It is no less so for chief executives.

There is so little accountability in social roles that you can learn how to perform acceptably. But those who arrive in high-level roles are often scrutinized. The President has naysayers. So do most CEOs.

The point is that few arrive in those roles with the competencies needed to perform well in them. More often than not, they are there to *learn how* to perform competently. Eventually, no matter how well they may have performed in their lower roles, many if not most will fail in the higher ones.

I have dealt with many CEOs who assumed they got the job because they were competent to perform it. So they felt they had little more to learn. They were wrong. They were placed in that role to *learn how* to perform it. But alas! Many were no longer capable of learning. So they failed.

As CEO coach Marshall Goldsmith might say, "What got you here will not get you *there*," meaning—to full competence in a role you have heretofore never been in.

So there is something very fundamental about Peters' cautionary maxim. It should guide anyone who steps into a high-level role in any organization.

Every new role has to be learned. Past experience in other roles will rarely carry the day.

Failure to understand that has caused many a failure at the executive level.

The competent organization—

has a compelling *cause*—a compelling and higher reason for existing.

Making money is necessary, because it is to organizations like blood or metabolism are to the human body. It's a need. But it is not a higher cause.

Organizations live or die in the myopic pursuit of money or size or power. None of those is a higher *cause* for existence.

The question is: "What is my organization FOR?" In the context of all the rest of the human project on earth, and in the context of your particular organization's role in the future of that project, what should you be trying to accomplish?

Some say that is not a very practical way to look at it. It's difficult to imagine anything more practical. All lives—including the lives of organizations—exist in the context of the evolving history of something higher.

For individuals, it is the relationships in which they have their immediate existence. Relationships exist in the context of groups or tribes or societies. And they exist in the context of the fate of humanity on earth. And so on.

That's what morality—*practical* morality—is all about. It is about having a cause that is greater than one is. It is about having a cause that contributes to better conditions and beliefs for everyone's existence, both now and in the future.

> *By definition, a competent organization is one that exists in perpetual pursuit of a purpose higher and broader than its own pecuniary ones.*

If you were to ask any member of the organization, or any of its stakeholders, "What is this organization FOR?" they could tell you exactly what their higher purpose is.

> *That, too, is a hallmark of a competent organization.*

A competent organization—

is one that has a **career**. It has a legacy that becomes a part of its culture and imbues future generations with the obligation to further that legacy.

["Career" is admittedly a metaphor. But there is no alternative when talking about an abstraction like an "organization." A marriage can be defined only by metaphor. It is the same with an organization.]

What we want to mean by a *career* here is that it is recognized by the larger public as having a purpose that they look upon favorably. A career has a beginning. It has a life of its own in the minds of others.

A career is either continuously growing. Or it is dying. There is no status quo where a career is concerned.

A *career* is thus akin to a *reputation*. It's not what you think of yourself. It's what other people think of you.

This is important, and useful. Mediocre or conventional organizations often define themselves internally. Competent organizations define themselves by how their stakeholders define them.

They monitor this continuously. If that definition is accurate, they change what has to be changed in order to pursue their cause. If it is wrong, the task is to change their reputation by doing what they should be doing in the eyes of their stakeholders.

> *Competent organizations know they can't be any better than their stakeholders believe them to be. They want their reputation to be fully aligned with what they are FOR. If it is amiss, they fix themselves.*

That is what careerists do.

The competent organization—

has a very different *culture*.

We have touched upon this before. But it is worth reconsidering.

- **The first point of which to be constantly mindful is that every organization leans in the direction of the majority of people who create and maintain it.**

So if the majority of people in your organization are no more than marginally-competent, the culture will select for more like them. It will nurture less rather than more competence. It will reward the mediocre—the marginally-competent. And it will punish in some way those who are most competent.

In other words, a culture that favors incompetence will dictate the future and the destiny of your organization—regardless of what you are trying to accomplish.

You could be moving uphill against a force which has more power than you do.

- **The second point is that what you have to develop to become a fully competent organization is a majority of the opposite kind of people.**

This is where most otherwise capable and rightly-intentioned chief executives fail. They can see the inescapable logic. But they don't know what to do about it.

It's simple enough, really. It's just very difficult to do in an existing context that probably opposes you.

- *You must make it **necessary**, in whatever way you can invent, for your existing people to become consistently more competent in their individual roles.*
- *Those who cannot or will not make the painful transition from incompetence to full competence in their roles must be eliminated.*

[Remember here the old saw: One bad apple in a basket will rot away all of the other apples in that basket. Farmers cannot tolerate the bad apple. Neither can you.]

- *Every new member of the organization must at least be more competent than the average of what you already have.*

Don't let the less-than-competent people select the newcomers. They will select people like they are. That's the squirrel cage.

You have to eliminate the less-than-competent performers at one end, while simultaneously adding people who can and will have to be more competent in those roles they are replacing.

While doing both of those things with laser-like attention and inventiveness, you must make it **necessary** for all of those still in place to become regularly more competent in their roles. This can be done only by making it necessary for them to develop the habits and the outlook of the learning mode.

You have to do this by measuring, not their competence today, but their gains in competence . . . continuously.

People who are not continuously getting better at what they do must be helped to find a competing organization in which to perpetrate their stagnation and spoil all of the apples in THAT organization.

There is no job in any organization which could not be done better tomorrow—and forever.

It is key to your role to make certain this happens—one way or another.

A competent organization—

is one in which people love what they do.

Whatever they do—from tending the surrounds of the organization to answering the phone, loading the truck, or pretending to run the place—is done attentively, with engagement, and with pride which cannot be denied in the outcome.

That may seem like a fairy tale. But it is not. It is as concrete as anything gets.

People who are competent at the work they do . . . do it with great and growing competence. They do it with conscientiousness. They do it with great care. They do it with engagement.

- *It is the competence of people that determines how much they embrace and love their work and its consequences.*

It is not something else. You cannot buy it or talk people into caring about their work. That depends *exclusively* on how competent they are at it.

People who are competent at what they do are ever-vigilant about how the consequences of their performance affect other people.

They are cognizant of the impact of their work on others, on their organization, on its stakeholders, and on the health and welfare of their society. Competent people have a much larger, more conscientious purview.

THE COMPETENT ORGANIZATION

People who love their work also care about the people who buy it or use it. In an organization of fully competent people, there is little need for "Customer Service." It is provided at the outset by everyone who has a hand in delivering the product or the service.

In a hospital, it is the most competent people who care most about the patients. In a school, it is the people who are most competent in their roles who really care about the students' learning and growth. In a repair shop, it is the most competent mechanics who care most about meeting their customers' automobile and psychological needs.

In an investment firm, it is the people who are most competent in their role who can really reach out and advantage their clients. It is only the most competent persons in a retail store who can provide the customer with the experience they came for.

It is the incompetent employees of an airline who daily provide travelers with bad experiences. It is only those who are fully competent in their own roles who can actually *care* about the users of the organization.

Competent individuals are necessary and indispensable to a would-be competent organization.

On the other hand, some competent people become too full of themselves to care about how their work affects others in the organization or its users. That just means that those few have ceased to be fully competent, since one of the characteristics of competent people is that they are forever in the process of becoming more competent.

They are in your organization to *learn how* to do this. If they are not continuously learning how to perform better, they are not competent, and should be dealt with summarily.

Only your most competent people can really *care* about your stakeholders—any who use your organization for their purposes.
They can "love" the people who are looking for them only because they love their work. And they can love their work only because they are increasingly competent in their role.

LEE THAYER

A competent organization—

is one that is healthy because it is not poisoned by incompetence. Competence is the source of a healthy organization. Incompetence is the source of an unhealthy organization.

An organization that is not healthy cannot be a competent organization, any more than an incompetent person can be robustly healthy.

Even a good idea carried out beyond its relevance can encourage incompetence. One of Peter's principles is as follows:

> *"Equal opportunity means everyone will have a fair chance of becoming incompetent."*

Equal opportunity was probably a good idea at one time. Equal opportunity should result in giving everyone a fair chance of becoming competent. But it doesn't seem to work that way.

For reasons known only to the gods of human nature, incompetence is far more infectious and contagious than competence. People can catch the incompetence bug just by sitting around. There seems to be no competence bug. If you want to be competent, you have to do it the hard way.

All you have to do to be incompetent is to avoid the hard way. AND, surround yourself with incompetent people.

If there were no incompetent people in the world, then hypothetically everyone might be competent. That's more than a bit utopian. With real world government policies and social norms that support and protect the incompetent, people are inclined to choose the normative way.

The lesson for anyone who wants to make a competent organization, the lesson is the contrary one:

Nurture competence wherever and whenever you encounter it. This requires you to be fully competent in your own role, in order to recognize it when you see it.

The Competent Organization

**Extinguish or punish incompetence wherever and whenever
you encounter it.
You have to be relentless if you intend to develop a competent
organization.
The less ruthless you are about either, the more incompetence
you will suffer.**

The competent organization—

if full of competent people who are innovators and inventers.

Not in the grand sense. But in the local sense. Competent people *invent* better
ways of doing their own work. They *innovate* in small ways on a daily basis.

If the procedures by which the internal communication systems work inhibit
their performance, they fix them. If they don't have work in which they can
engage themselves and push their own boundaries, they fix that. If they have
a boss who is incompetent, they fix that—either by making it necessary for
that boss to become more and more competent, or by dumping him or her.

They are revolutionaries in the cause of greater competence—both for
themselves and for their organization.

Since competent people know when to lead, when to follow, and when to
get the h!## out of the way, they police themselves. If there is no obvious
way forward, they are capable of inventing one. If time is wasted, they
innovate a way of making that less and less possible.

They expect a good return (in their performance) from their attention. If
they don't get it, they either fix themselves or the conditions of their work.

They know they cannot be fully competent in an incompetent organization.
They will innovate until they find a way of fixing that. They know they themselves
can't get well in a sick organization. They either fix that, or they leave.

Competent people may not be liked by those who are less competent. But
they command a premium in the job market. So they have more freedom
of choice. Incompetent people have to take what they can get.

If that's a position in an organization that is no more than marginally competent, they have to take what they can get.

People avoid competence because it requires commitment and hard work. Better, incompetent people believe, to take whatever happens to come along. People striving to be more competent can fail. If a person is not striving, there is no failure.

Unless, of course, you recall Martha Graham's comment about the only sin. Which is what? Mediocrity.

A competent organization—

is one that is intolerant of sloth, of indifference, of welfare for the able-bodied, and of prejudice against competent people.

A person who is not getting better is getting worse. If the status quo provides a safe haven for incompetent people in your organization, you have sealed the fate of your organization.

The more incompetence you tolerate, even for the best of reasons, the more of that you will get. Incompetent people, like incompetent organizations, are short-sighted. They measure their comfort by asking "What have you done for ME today?

It seems that incompetent people are inadvertent *evangelists* for their way of life. It is a way of life that is always less than it could be. Meanwhile, competent people do not want others to default themselves. They know where a better life lies. They are disciples. But they are not evangelists for even a better life.

Competent people measure their progress by what they have done for their organizations today. And by how much more they will be able to contribute tomorrow.

And that translates directly into what the competent organization can do for its users today . . . and tomorrow and tomorrow.

To be continued . . .

THE COMPETENT ORGANIZATION

". . . you can know everything there is to know about business and still be a lousy manager."—Charles Handy

7.   The Competent Organization: III

Incompetence seems to be a bit like the weather. Everyone talks about it, but no one does anything about it.

A rare exception is Laurence Peter. He wrote a few books about it (for example, *The Peter Principle*, dealt with in the previous chapter). His books spawned dozens of others. Still, all that was just talk, as pertinent as it may have been.

Let us ponder this one, from his book *When Things Go Wrong* (1984):

"Incompetence knows no barriers of time or place."

Clever . . . But how ought we to comprehend this as an aspect of designing and constructing competent *organizations*?

- Competence belongs to a particular time and place. When Joshua Bell, who can fill concert halls, played his Stradivarius in the subway, he was snubbed. There's a time and place for competence.

- But incompetence rears its ugly head everywhere, at any time. We are confronted with incompetence on a daily basis. It is most likely the cause "when things go wrong."

So they reveal themselves differently. We have expectations about competence. But we don't buy a ticket to experience incompetence. It befalls us uninvited.

Here's how we might most advantageously comprehend this difference:

> *People who use organizations for their purposes have certain expectations. They are put off—angered, disappointed, or frustrated when their expectations are foiled.*

> *If we expected incompetence—almost always the cause of our expectations being foiled—if we expected incompetence, but were treated quite competently, we would be surprised and stunned.*

It is competence that is rare. We ply our worlds in a heightening swamp of incompetence. It would be difficult if not impossible to out-compete incompetence. But organizations seem to try it every day.

Organizations attempt to emulate other organizations. So they all end up being . . . mediocre, which is to say with incompetence designed in.

Certainly copycat organizations do something cosmetically to distinguish themselves. But these tricks are not fundamental differences. As Lincoln said, you can fool some of the people some of the time, but you can't fool all of the people all of the time.

Even incompetent people sometimes recognize and resent incompetence when they are the victim.

A very practical point to prompt some action:

> **It requires *two* competent people to compensate for the shortfalls of *one* incompetent person in an organization: One to do half of the incompetent person's work; and the other to provide for the incompetent person's economic contribution shortfall.**

At the same time, you have lost some of the direct contribution that could have been made by the two competent people who get drawn in to compensate for those shortfalls. Why does it take three or more people to discuss a problem that should not have occurred in the first place?

The Competent Organization

Since most of the mistakes, errors, and problems are created by incompetent people, it is clear that **incompetence is the largest single cost factor bearing on the performance of most conventional organizations.**

The competent organization—

is one whose MO is inductive and not deductive.

Incompetent people need far more support than do competent people. That's because competent people acquire the intelligence (sometimes called "information") and the resources they need, on an as-needed basis. They don't have to be provided with a cookie-cutter set of procedures.

Bureaucracies and bureaucratic procedures grow in support of incompetent or marginally-competent people. Those are *deductive*. They attempt to foresee what role-incumbents will need in this or that situation, and provide that person with the answers.

If you have ever dealt with the automated phone system of a bureaucratic organization, you know that you can baffle the system by asking any simple question. The system is not geared to serve you and *your* problems. It is there to compensate for the failure to hire or to develop competent personnel.

An organization is operating *inductively* when competent people know where to get the information or the resources they need to perform in their roles. Organizations become "top-heavy" because they need all of that heavy-handedness to support the activities of incompetent people.

People who are question-askers are operating *inductively*.

A competent organization—

is one that is comprised of *bricoleurs*. Bricoleurs are competent people who accomplish what needs to be accomplished with the tools and the resources at hand.

They are engaged in what is called *bricolage*. This is one part triage and two parts resourcefulness.

This is closely related to the previous point.

Competent people simply need less supervision, and they need far less staff support. In one organization, for example, as the people who did the work of the organization became increasingly competent, the sheer amount of the levels of supervision and the staff support they needed shrank proportionally.

That organization won twice. Better performance at less cost. Or, as we might say today, it was a matter of doing more with less. The answer lies in competence, not in some glitzy new management gimmick.

Bureaucracies were made for marginally-incompetent people. And marginally-incompetent people are made for bureaucracies. You can identify the competent people. Bureaucratic processes drive them crazy. Incompetent people feel right at home.

Bureaucracy is the enemy of competent organizations, as Percy Barnevik said when he was CEO of ABB. But you can't kill bureaucracy unless you dig out its roots. That requires transforming the organization into a competent one. It doesn't help to overlay it with some popular new idea.

Less-than-competent organizations cannot be fixed at the top—or by the "experts." They have to be fixed where the action is. And the "fix" is increasing competence in every role.

There is no fairy-dust. There is no magic bullet. There is no panacea. It all comes down to basic competence—oft-overlooked but the only sustainable advantage to any organization.

A competent organization—

is one in which competent people say what they mean and mean what they say.

We've visited this before. But it deserves revisiting.

Saying what you mean requires you to actually know what you mean—both how you intend to be interpreted and what you are attempting to accomplish.

Meaning what you say requires you first to follow-up. If others don't get it, make sure you know going in what the consequences for them are if they don't.

This may require you to be more articulate and wholly in control of your mind and your mouth than you are accustomed to.

There is no excuse, no alternative. You have to understand what you mean before you say it. And you have to know what the consequences are if others don't understand you.

You have to be good at your part of it if you expect others to be good at their part of it. For others to know that you mean what you say, you have to have that kind of reputation. You can't gain that in a day or a week. You have to make it a habit.

When it works that way every time, it will become a part of the culture of your organization. The culture will then do the heavy lifting for you.

A competent organization—

is one in which competent people don't talk about what "ought" to be done. They just do it.

Competent people are doers, not talkers. A competent organization needs to be the same way. Don't talk about who you are or what you intend to do. Just do the right thing and let the result speak for itself.

Every new communications tool has increased the amount of chatter leading nowhere in particular. Twitter, anyone?

Competent people do not much use their cell phones or computers. Like Edison, they have no "rules." They just want to get things done. And a chat room is not a place where things get done.

Neither is a meeting. Great organizations have been built without large gatherings to determine a course of action. People may come equipped with their spreadsheets or their power point presentations. But no amount of data ever revealed what needed to be done.

Incompetent people hide behind data. Or behind what they "know." Competent people do not attempt to parade their superior knowledge. They prefer simply doing what needs doing rather than engaging in contests to see who "knows" the most.

What "ought" to be done is never buried in masses of data. What "ought" to be done is a choice. It is a choice about the right next steps in the direction of the organization's *cause*.

Competent people blaze a trail forward. Incompetent people take the road most traveled.

> *The difference between talk and action is most often the difference between notable success and puzzling failure.*

The competent organization—

raises the quality of life of all of those members who feel responsible for the organization's cause and thus its future.

An incompetent organization diminishes the lives of all who work there—including especially the chief executive. It is after all the preeminent task of every organization's leaders to make their organizations measurably more competent on a continuing basis . . . forever.

The best measure of increased and increasing competence is that you can feel it. It is one of those things you have to experience to understand it. That it is not measured is a function of the (mainly) financial tools at hand, not of its importance.

Every competent organization can measure it in *esprit des corps*, in fewer health and mental health issues, and in the sheer joy that comes from being stretched to become more competent.

Competent people measure life in terms of worthy accomplishments. So should competent organizations.

Incompetent organizations measure life in terms of "the numbers." So do the incompetent people who measure themselves in terms of the numbers.

> *Competent fishermen know how to catch fish. Incompetent fishermen just "go fishing" with a tub of beer. Metaphorically, it is the same for organizations.*

What is the measure of "quality of life"? Ask those who have made it so. Do not ask those who want it handed to them. There is no way they can understand it.

The competent organization—

cannot be copied. It is one of a kind. They are as different from one another as they are from the run-of-the-mill conventional (or mediocre) organization.

Conventional organizations are easy to copy. That's why we have so many of them.

But merely **doing** what competent organizations do misses the real ingredients. You cannot make a competent organization out of incompetent people, no matter how hard you try.

You cannot raise the performance of people in your organization by trying to incentivize them—either with dollars or with words. That's because the existing culture of the organization is more powerful than they are—and more powerful than any guru's recipes.

A great organization is a byproduct of its culture—whether it is the Marines, the Salvation Army, Southwest Airlines, or the Mafia.

How people think about their role in an organization, and how they perform it, is a function of that particular organization's particular culture. That cannot be copied.

There is no "Shazam!" where a culture is concerned. It is a distillation of beliefs, values, and life lessons over a long period of time. And it is a living thing, constantly evolving.

You cannot manipulate it. But you can change it little by little to support and underwrite your cause. So it all begins with just how competent you and all of your key people are in your respective roles. It cannot be made tangible. It exists only in the minds of your people and your stakeholders.

The right one comes from how virtuous your accomplishments are, and how competently those accomplishments were achieved.

"Virtuous" here is the root for *virtuosity*. That is not measured by how much money you make. It is measured by whether or not you set the new standard for the performance of other organizations by how remarkable your accomplishments are.

Great organizations live or die by their accomplishments. And by how they redefined the basics to bring those accomplishment off. It is remarkable but fundamental competence that produces great accomplishments.

> *You get there one person at a time, one process at a time, and one day at a time, as Shackleton learned.*

A competent organization—

makes all of its users and its stakeholders—and even its competitors—*better* as a result of every contact they have with that organization.

In the same way that competent servers make more competent diners, competent organizations raise the level of all of their users' competence. They do this just by sheer contact and transaction. People perform at a higher level when they are surrounded by competence. People perform at a lower level when they are surrounded by incompetence—which, regrettably, is most often the case these days.

Users always have something of value to learn about performing their own roles by getting involved with competent organizations. And that kind of relationship continuously renews itself because competent organizations are full of people who are continuously learning how to get better at everything they do.

Competitors gain because they have to improve just to keep up. Suppliers gain because competent organizations require improved performance.

Members of the organization gain because, as we have seen, *learning = growth = more life.*

Some schools are better than others because they have more competent and dedicated teachers, and more competent and dedicated students. Some hospitals are better because they have more competent personnel in every *role*, and this contributes to more competent patients, suppliers, etc.

Some airlines are better than others because they deliver the experiences that customers expect. They can do this only with competent employees in every role, and with the kind of logistics that enable competent people to be even more competent—as we will see.

Competent organizations enrich the quality of life in the communities where they operate, and in society in general. Competent organizations are healthier, which contributes to greater health for their members and for the economy as a whole.

Competent organizations raise the bar. Although they are raising the bar primarily to propel themselves to greater competence, it raises the bar for their contemporaries and for others who come after them but aspire to the level of their performance.

All this would be true, of course, if it were not for the fact that in the larger culture, we have come to expect incompetence—barely acceptable performance, surliness, indifference, carelessness, and all the rest.

> *Wherever expectations decline, performance declines. That's because where performance declines, our at-large expectations seem to follow.*

The only antidote is the competent organization. One competent organization will not turn around this awful downward spiral unto the degradation of what our social destiny *might* otherwise be.

But thousands of them would.

A competent organization—

is accomplishment-minded. It is not activity-minded. If the activity does not contribute to an accomplishment, it must be eliminated.

The competent people who comprise a competent organization are always up to something that moves everything along in the direction of the organization's cause(s) in life. A competent organization is one that always appears to be up to something—because it is.

A competent organization is an audacious organization. While it is always frugal and conservative financially, it is willing to bet on itself. That's because it knows what it is capable of. Mistakes of judgment are often made by marginally-competent organizations because they can only guess at (or hope for) what it is capable of.

A competent organization is one that measures above all else what is being paid attention to throughout the organization, from top to bottom and from side to side. What is being measured is **Return On Attention (ROA)**.

This is a measure of what we are getting in return for what we devote our attention to—a measure that is implicitly used by competent people.

It is used almost exclusively by competent organizations. Incompetent or marginally-competent (mediocre) organizations seem to be unaware or not care about this investment—the most precious and irrecoverable investment that a person or an organization can make.

Reading a book or a report, reading and answering emails, talking on the phone or the hallway or in meetings: all of these and everything else that people do with their attention represents an irrecoverable cost. For a competent organization, it is the primary measure of vigor, vitality, and purpose.

Whatever is expected can be rationalized. What is not expected cannot be rationalized in advance. It can be dealt with only by heightened competence. For incompetent organizations, these kinds of unmeasured sunk costs are astronomical.

> *People who staff competent organizations smile a lot.*
> *They know why. Others can only wonder.*

LEE THAYER

"The most important marketer in our company is the man or woman on the loading dock who decides not to drop the damned box into the back of the truck." [Executive of a high-tech company, cited in Peters and Austin, *A Passion for Excellence*.]

8. The Competent Organization: IV

Back in 1987, the remarkable then-President of Scandinavian Airlines (SAS), Jan Carlzon, published a book entitled *Moments of Truth*. The epigram above refers indirectly but just as importantly to what he meant by a "moment of truth."

As Carlzon put it (on pp. 2-3):

> *"SAS is not a collection of material assets but the quality of the contact between an individual customer and the SAS employees who serve the customer directly . . .*
> *Last year, each of our 10 million customers came in contact with five SAS employees, and this contact lasted an average of 15 seconds each time. Thus, SAS is 'created' 50 million times a year . . . These 50 million 'moments of truth' are the moments that ultimately determine whether SAS will succeed or fail as a company,"*

It could hardly be stated more succinctly. We need only add that the "moments of truth" for any organization also include contact with suppliers, with employees, and with every other stakeholder or user of that organization.

Those contacts will be judged by all of those who "use" the organization in some way as competent . . . or not. The experience that any user expected or hoped-for will either be fulfilled . . . or not.

The "users" of any organization—no matter how far removed they may be from any actual employee—will judge their overall experience with that organization. If the damned box was dropped in the back of the truck, they will know. Any direct or indirect experience with that organization will color their image of that organization. It becomes a vital part of how that user sees and thinks about that organization.

The best marketing you can buy derives from the interpretations of your stakeholders and users. That's the bedrock.

You will never have enough money to pay for the marketing or PR required to compensate for poor or negative "moments of truth." In fact, most of those attempts will be payment to *make up for* negative "moments of truth." Positive "moments of truth" would have been far cheaper and far more advantageous.

Few members of our contemporary organizations don't see it that way. They are busy thinking about products, about cutting costs, and about the problems that arise from negative moments of truth.

Customer service personnel are taught to say something like, "Your call is important to us." How "important" it actually is . . . depends on how long you are left hanging on the line.

There are many old proverbs about doing it right in the first instance, For example,

> *A stitch in time saves nine.*

What's done right the first time saves all of the agonizing time and effort required to "fix" a problem caused by some careless inattention.

And money. If it costs 9 times as much to *fix* something that could have been done right the first time, that's quite a spread. Investment in increasing competence is always a good investment.

Most of the unattributed costs in running any organization are the costs of the consequences of incompetence. Eliminate incompetence and you have eliminated the source of those costs.

The competent organization—

is a customer- or client-driven organization. The best military units are driven by their adversaries. So we would want to add that the competent organization is driven by its cause or its reason for being, AND by its competitors, its employees, and its other stakeholders.

Carlzon offers one slice of that:

> *"In a customer-driven company, the distribution of roles is radically different. The organization is decentralized, with responsibility delegated to those who until now have comprised the order-obeying bottom level of the pyramid."*

He is saying that if you turn the conventional organization chart upside down, you would be looking at the way the organization *should* be functioning.

In order for this to work even adequately requires that those people who are now responsible have to be far more competent in that *role* than they have been in their typical roles.

If you decentralize, you put front-line units in business for themselves. There are few employees in the typical organization who are capable of running the business—or even participating effectively in these decentralized units.

This means you have to create what have sometimes been called "intrapreneurs"—that is, internal entrepreneurs. Without greatly heightened and enlarged competencies, most members of most organizations cannot function in decentralized units—in what might be referred to as "mini-businesses."

As close as we have come to this in the contemporary world is to organize around project teams and project team managers. Usually the responsibility for the *expected* performance of the "team" is higher up in the traditional pyramid.

I believe that Carlzon's observations are insightful, and correct. His analysis is useful. But the Scandinavian culture is not the American culture. Even though organizations like Southwest Airlines and USAA and L L Bean and Nordstrom's have been able to *partially* move in this direction, it is mostly just a provocative idea for most leaders.

It is still the same distance between the idea and its implementation that has always faced the leaders of organizations. How to *do* that?

Some reliable prerequisites for accomplishing what Carlzon envisioned are set forth in Part III. But we first have to add to our mental provisions some additional perspectives on just what constitutes a competent organization.

A competent organization—

is one that is continuously engaged in *due diligence*. There are several key aspects to this:

- One is that conventional organizations pay attention only when a problem arises. Competent organizations pay attention *before* a problem arises.
- They have the habits and the systems for providing themselves with "intelligence" about anything going on within the organization or in its present or future environments that might bear upon their pursuit of their mission in life.
- They know that *continual* surveillance of anything that might bear upon their performance today and tomorrow is what matters.
- They also know that this cannot be a matter of collecting data or "information." All data and all "information" has to be interpreted. They have people and procedures for interpreting this data, in whatever domain it occurs.
- Competent organizations have people who are competent to sort out the wheat from the chaff. They know what to look for and how to determine its relevance—how to render it *meaningful*.
- Those competent people also have efficacious systems for alerting those in the organization who have a need to know.
- As pointed out earlier, competent people are also engaged in performing real time triage on emerging events and trends. That is, they know how to discern and how to communicate threats and opportunities, etc.

- They follow through. If something relevant needs to be dealt with, competent people assume responsibility for getting it done—all the way to a positive outcome.
- It is critical to know what the salient circumstances are at all times. It is equally critical to know what needs to be accomplished in the present and in the long-term future. Competent organizations do not take snapshots. They live in a continuous reel from their beginnings to their chosen destiny.
- "Profit" is important. But far more important is a mindset throughout the competent organization of *profitability*.
- Competent organizations operate on the belief that every transaction within the organization and between the organization and its users must make a positive contribution to the health and welfare of the organization.
- Competent organizations operate on the inescapable logic that says what doesn't make a positive contribution makes a negative contribution. There are no "break-even" contributions.

Competent people know how to engage continuously in due diligence. If they didn't, there could not be competent organizations.

A competent organization—

is one that is frugal, but bold and audacious.

That's because, unlike conventional organizations, they are justified in betting on themselves, and not relying solely on external events.

They do not rely on "luck." They rely on themselves.

Competent people take risks. But they take only those risks they are competent to bring to fruition—whatever the obstacles, whatever happens along the way. They take *calculated* risks—where their competence is the biggest part of the calculation.

Competence succeeds when there is no obvious way of succeeding.

Organizations fail because they overestimate their competencies. Competent organizations are realistic. They know what they are capable of and what they are not capable of. It is their misjudgments about their competencies that lead organizations to failure.

Being more than competent carries with it the frugality. Being less than competent creates unforeseen problems. Being more than competent deflects those problems—or at least reveals them in advance.

Boldness has its own impact. Incompetent organizations are very cautious, for good reason. Competent organizations can afford to be bold, and thus grasp the advantage of boldness.

Competent organizations dominate by their boldness. Positive outcomes are more likely given the competencies they always have in reserve.

Without the competence to act in just the right way at the right time, conventional organizations are at risk. It is only competent organizations that can afford the risk.

Competent organizations—

do not rely on a singular "leader"—no matter what kind of charisma or other "leader" *qualities* he or she is purported to have. The "leader" may be the one the media and thus the public puts on the stage. But extraordinary organizations require much more than a "leader."

Competent organizations are full from top to bottom and side to side of **stewards**— stewards of the organization's mission, today, tomorrow and beyond.

Every competent person in a competent organization is a steward of that organization's daily life, health, and destiny. It is that critical mass that propels competent organizations—not the ideas or antics of one "leader."

That is what is missing in marginally-incompetent organizations: widespread stewardship. It is something that can be had only when the organization is full of competent people.

It is not so much "being on the same page" as *sharing* the authorship of the organization's story.

A great and worthy purpose—or reason for being—may be articulated by the organization's "leader." But unless most of the people in that organization are *stewards* of that purpose or reason for being, it will not come to pass.

A competent organization—

is one that is measurably better at *diagnosing* situations and problems.

We seem to assume that "experience" brings with it superior capabilities as competent diagnosticians. *That's an assumption you never want to make.* The two—experience and the ability to diagnose present problems—are two very different things.

In the first place, *experience* is always circumstantial. Luck and happenstance are *always* components of past experience. You can size up a situation wrongly, but still be successful. You can size up a situation rightly, but still fail.

In that sense, "experience" is always a bit of a red herring.

The learned capacity for diagnosing situations and problems becomes a unique competency that every organization needs. Carlzon's "Moments of Truth" depend entirely on how the situation or problem is interpreted. Identifying moments of truth does not get those critical interactions solved intelligently or comprehensively.

Repeating one's experience from the past is no guarantor of success in the present. The circumstances are never the same. Merely applying experience doesn't always work. It is, in fact, a form of blindness. Unless people train themselves to deny their natural tendencies, they will see what they *expect* to see.

In her book, *Every Patient Tells a Story*, which is really about "the art of diagnosis," Lisa Sanders examines in great detail and with the help of much research why so many doctors are not very good at diagnosing. Part of the problem is that patients are not very good at describing. But not every medical problem has an obvious answer to the question, "Why?"

Neither do problems in ordinary life. There are symptoms, but people do not expose or reveal them well. No problem comes to us with its relevance or its solution inscribed on its back.

This is no less so for any problem an organization faces.

They arise. And people have to interpret them. And every interpretation is at least one human pronouncement removed from the facts.

What typically happens is that the *symptoms* are treated, based on past experience. An accurate diagnosis has to use the symptoms to get at what is behind them—what is hidden beneath them, what is actually *causing* them.

The fictional Sherlock Holmes is iconic for his remarkable detective work. He thinks his way into the world and the mind of the criminal. He gets there by looking at "the evidence." But he knows it is the mind of the criminal that is pertinent—not the obvious evidence.

The diagnostician may try to be very rational in approach. But the "cause" of any problem facing organizations is rarely rational. So the diagnostician must be capable of meeting the cause on its own ground—that being the irrational.

Outside the laboratory, there are rarely simple causes of simple effects.

There may be multiple causes. And they do not always present the same symptoms.

That's why competent organizations rely on diagnostic competencies and not on problem-"solvers." That's why competent organizations rely on competent diagnosticians rather than "experience."

Competent people are superior diagnosticians. They have to be. It comes with the territory. Incompetent people, like incompetent organizations, rely on past experience. And that's why they end up putting a band-aid on the symptoms. They don't know how to get at the causes that, once identified, will preclude the problem from happening again and again.

The closer to the ultimate causes you can get, the better able you are to *preclude* problems. This is the aim of competent organizations—either to anticipate or to preclude.

For example, the most likely cause of most problems *in* organizations is incompetence. Marginally-competent organizations either do not see this.

Or they neglect it because they can't imagine what can be done about this kind of underlying problem.

Another example: most problems involving customers (or clients) comes from the fact that the former have expectations, but organizations have "policies." Those come from two different worlds. You can't have a love affair with customers, or they with you, if you live in two different worlds. You have to have common cause. And that would be the expectations—or the actual needs—of your customers.

Or it might be your indispensability to them. Who needs who the most?

Competent organizations make themselves indispensable to their users/ stakeholders/personnel.

Competent organizations—

are those rare organizations that engage routinely in enabling—down, up, and all around.

Competent people are always ready and helpful teachers and mentors, willing to help anyone who asks and is open to learning. Competent organizations will even reach out to their stakeholders—even their competitors, if asked, to help them become more competent.

They know that more competent competitors will make it necessary for them to become even more competent themselves. They welcome the best challenges.

The underlying thrust of competence is to enable a person—or an organization—to become even more competent. In the same way, learning has as its most desirable product not "knowledge" as such, but an increased and increasing capacity for more learning.

Real learning enables elevated performance. Learning that does not enable elevated performance is wasted.

And it takes competence to gain competence. There are no outside forces capable of making a person or an organization smarter or more capable, except that to which competent people are open.

Competent people know—as it was known 2500 years ago—that you cannot confer a benefit on an unwilling person (or an unwilling organization).

You can't make someone more competent against his or her will. It is also the case that you cannot make an organization more competent unless it is capable.

Competent organizations have two potent advantages:

- *They are always in the process of becoming more competent, and*
- *They welcome any challenge or problem that might enhance their competencies.*

They are driven by the need to accomplish. Less than competent organizations are driven by past habits and routines that are obsolete and rigidly protective of the status quo.

9. The Competent Leader's Role

We should not be remiss here. *Competent* leadership *does* have a role—a *key* role. But that is in making a *competent* organization, not "running" a conventional organization—no matter what their aspirations or claims.

We have come to use the word "leader" to refer to anyone who seems to be in charge of any kind of organization or project. Used carelessly in this way denigrates the use of the term.

To make the concept more useful and more powerful, it helps at the outset to abandon the term "leader" to refer to a person. It is not the person we should be studying. It is the process of **leadership** that we should be studying. What is it that great leadership has contributed to the legacy of that process?

A "leader" is not a person who merely administers or manages things. Competent leaders make their indispensable contributions either in advance or concomitantly with all that.

There is considerable ambivalence—even fuzziness—about the concept of leadership. There needn't be. If competent leaders make indispensable contributions to outcomes, they would have to be unique. They would have to characterize leadership contributions differentiated from all others.

So our aims in this chapter are these two:

- To isolate the contributions to the outcomes that can only be made by leadership; and
- By doing this, returning to the term "leadership" the kind of meaning that rightfully and uniquely belongs to it.

The fundamental tasks of *competent* leadership

The unique contributions of competent leadership come from the creative and strategic implementation of its basic tasks. There are three of these foundational tasks:

- The first is that of making a competent *organization*.
- The second, *people-making*.
- And the third, making the *meanings* that congeal and propel the organization on its rightful trajectory at all times.

We will want to delve into these three tasks of *competent* leadership in some detail below.

Task 1: Organization-making—continuously composing and recomposing a fully competent organization

There is no logical need for understanding leadership apart from the organization in which it is to be practiced.

True, there are people in the arts and the sciences—and even in golf—who change the game, put it on a different trajectory. How they do what they do redefines that role for others who follow them. Their performance in their role sets the bar.

This is influence. Those who look up to them may be doing so in order to better perform in that role. Or they may simply be acolytes—those who want to identify with or emulate celebrity thinkers or performers.

As the historian Daniel Boorstin once said, "People are well-known for being well-known." Following them for that reason won't get you very far.

Most people do not want to trouble themselves to be outstanding performers or change-makers. They just want to be seen as identifying with those who are outstanding performers or change-makers. Academics cite what they take to be those who are most celebrated for their theories or other pronouncements. Fans follow their favorite teams or music groups.

The people who are being followed are influential because there are lots of other people who want to be seen as their fans or acolytes. We followers want to be known for attaching ourselves through adulation to the best-known public figures of our interests.

These are not "leaders." Nor do they typically practice leadership. They are not necessarily trying to do good for the society or for their fans. They are in it for what *they* can get out of it in terms of money or status or fame. These are not "leaders."

They are not leaders, because they are not pursuers of great or worthy purposes for the larger whole.

Leadership raises people up. It does not pander to the lowest common denominator for its own purposes.

Families or friends or those who have power may lead people astray. This does not make them leaders. They are merely screwing up other people's lives. This is the opposite of real leadership.

The only justifiable reason for the study of leadership is that you have an organization that you intend to make competent—or to make *more* competent. All other reasons denigrate the term.

So we know that one of the first tasks of leadership is to create a competent organization. It would probably be useful to consider some provocative metaphors to grasp what's at stake in "creating" an organization.

Composers, for example, create symphonies or sonatas or just plain tunes. They start with an idea. They contemplate what effect they want to achieve with varying voices, harmonics, tempo, etc. Writers create novels or short stories. They imagine the story they want to tell, and then compose it. Pugilists imagine how they might defeat an opponent and then create the moves and deceits to do it. Lovers create a relationship and an environment for consummation. Artists imagine how the finished painting ought to appeal—to them and to their viewers. Then they create it.

The constant in all of these and similar creations is that of starting with nothing and finishing with something that demonstrates their virtuosity. Every writer starts with a blank screen or a blank sheet of paper. Given their own limitations and happenstance that they do not control, a product of their imaginations emerges.

It is something akin to this process that is involved in creating a competent organization.

Or . . . houses get designed. Buildings get designed. Ships get designed. Their infrastructure and façades are designed by architects. Everything has a structure—its architectonics—that has to be designed in some way.

Organizations are in basis the way things get articulated between its parts and between them and their environments.

> So *what needs to be designed or composed is not the structure of the organization as such—but how its components need to articulate (function) in such a way that it is forever on its path from where it is to the fulfillment of its mission.*

Every interaction, every transaction, is a "moment of truth." Every part of a symphony moves it along in the direction of the overall experience of it.

In other words,

How does an organization need to be *engineered* to produce its desired results?

Most organizations—certainly most conventional organizations—are created and built along the lines of the way existing organizations are designed and put together. They are hierarchical, they strive to be command-and-control, and they have certain "functions," like finance, human resources, operations, marketing, etc.

Each of these morphs into a silo. Each is a little fiefdom that protects its territory and covets more. They actually prefer to *function* somewhat autonomously. They have their own interests and their own subcultures which may be at odds with the aims of the organization as a whole.

It is always easier to communicate within those subcultures than between them. Most do not overlap with the organization's most indispensable stakeholders—like its customers or clients and its overall work force.

Let's say that you wanted to compose a customer-centric organization. What this requires is that anyone (or any technology) that has any contact at all with customers has to be competent to connect the interests of the customers with the interests of the organization. For the most part, there are very few people who even know that this *is* a key aspect of their role in the organization, let alone exhibit competence in fulfilling that role.

First of all, if you want to have a customer-centric organization (which most seem to aspire to), every person who has any direct or indirect contact with any customer has to be competent as a customer-service person. And I mean that in the most ideal way, not the way it is practiced today.

> *There is no tool or technique which can be any more effective than the person wielding it.*

> *Those persons must indeed be well-informed and armed with the intelligence they need to perform their roles superbly.*

> *But it isn't the technique or the information or the "intelligence" that converts that "moment of truth" into a real contribution to the organization's health and welfare. It is the competence of the person in the heat of the transaction.*

Technologies will not substitute for real performance. They can aid performance. But they cannot create performance. *"Listen carefully to the menu options"* is not serving a stakeholder. It is serving the organization.

THE COMPETENT ORGANIZATION

In the recent past, technologies have been applied to compensate for the incompetence of the people who staff the organization. In the Middle Ages, merchants made complicated calculations in their heads. Today, employees don't know how to make change. So the company buys an expensive cash register to do this for them.

They become bureaucratic—rule-followers, not actively engaged in their role at work. This is not progress. This is regress.

> When incompetence drives the design of an organization, the organization cannot itself become competent.

When you have to design an organization for incompetent people, it has to be fairly rigid and bureaucratic. Competent people have reserves. They know how to improvise. They are trying to accomplish something. That dedicated pursuit will lead to greater competence.

Any organization that does exactly the same thing today as it did yesterday is not a competent organization. If it were, it would have improved its processes, its performance.

> **Competence is not something people or organizations "have." It is not a destination or a fixed achievement.**
> **It is characterized by continuous improvement in performance.**
> **It is a learning journey that leads mainly to the capacity to perform better today than yesterday.**

People are not born competent. Organizations cannot be designed or composed to be fully competent at the outset or anywhere along their paths. Competence is simply a way of life. It is far different from its opposite.

Competent organizations are simply committed to getting better, every day, at everything they do.

That's how they intend to be perceived and measured.

They have a culture that makes this kind of commitment and performance *necessary*. It is a way of life that extends from yesterday into tomorrow and to all of the tomorrows after that. The present is merely a place for *learning* how to perform *better*.

It is not the competent leader's task to mandate this. It is his or her task to make it so, by every means.

|*Systems.*

The issue here is ultimately about systems *thinking* vs. cause-and-effect *thinking*. Cause-and-effect thinking is the way most people think. It is the conventional way of thinking in our culture.

It may be useful—if often misleading—in a laboratory. But the real world is comprised of *systems*. Things are connected to other things—the past to the present, the happenings that occur, we to each other mentally and emotionally—both because we imitate one another, or are beholden to one another.

Everything occurs in a system and in how that system is embedded in other systems, up and down, side to side. If we don't look at things in terms of their complex interconnectedness, we miss seeing the underlying pushes and pulls in the real world.

There is unlikely to be a single "cause" for anything.
And the "same" causes can produce different effects.
That's because everything occurs in a context—in a *system*.

Here's a brief on Systems 101:

- Every organization—even a two-person relationship—is a *system*.
- Every complex system is embedded in a nest of superior systems and has its own subsystems (subordinate systems).
- Every system has "nodes" that do processing or do work. In a human system (the only kind we'll talk about here), the "nodes" are people.
- The great leaders of history have all been systems thinkers. They looked at the world as a continuum and side to side in all of its interconnectedness.
- You may try to dictate the form and the ramifications of your organization. This is what leaders do, keeping in mind that

sidewalks do not keep people from "cutting across" and creating their own walkways.

- Competent people will over time create their own personal systems. Less-than-competent people will adjust to whatever systems they happen to fall into.
- There are "dumb systems" and then there are "smart systems." Dumb systems make optimum performance impossible. Smart systems facilitate optimum performance.
- The systems your systems are embedded in both enable and constrain them.
- The systems in which you live your everyday life enable certain possibilities and constrain or make unimaginable other possibilities.
- As you think, and thus as you *are,* and as you do are indirectly manipulated by the personal systems you inhabit.

This may seem to be saying no more than that the culture and subcultures you belong to are the source and the indirect manipulators of the way you think, of who you become, and how you perform yourself—how you choose and what you do—in the real world.

That's reasonable. But the concept of systems can be more potent. All systems are *communication* systems. And communication systems are the makers of minds, beliefs, feelings, perspectives, and explanations.

This makes conceiving of them more accessible and changing them more possible. The cultures and subcultures to which we belong will go far toward determining who we are and who we (*can*) become. Apart from radically changing our memberships in them, that doesn't give us much in the way of a tangible way of maneuvering.

To see them as *communication* systems does. As we communicate, and as we choose to be communicated-with will, when they are our *only* linkages with other minds, determine who we are, how we think, and what we will and will not do.

How competent you are as a lover or a CEO will depend upon the way your mind works. And the way your mind works will determine how competent you *can* become as a leader.

LEE THAYER

Systems both enable and constrain what can be done within them.

The genius of Toyota's manufacturing years back was that the people embedded in the line could stop the line from moving and initiate changes. The further advantage of this way of composing that part of the organization was that changes that could improve the processes involved could be made quickly and at the source of the problem.

Let's say that the car was painted before it was in final assembly. That was a good idea. But it also made it possible to scratch the paint inadvertently while assembling the car. When this happened, the worker who noticed it stopped the line (which was a system of repetitive communication between the present state of the car being produced and the people working on it).

Anyone could stop the line for purposes of improving the continuous process. Here was the ultimate insight:

- A worker could improve upon his or her personal performance at will, as long as it didn't impact any other process upstream or downstream.
- If it was a change that *might* affect another's work up- or down-stream, that person or team would have to be consulted about the change.
- If it was a change that *would* impact the overall system in some significant way, there has to be a meeting involving the leader of the line.
- If it impacts other processes in the organization—up, down, or laterally—those that would be impacted had to participate in the decision to change.

No more than common sense. But most conventional organizations are not designed in this way.

A competent leader would have designed it in that way, because competent leaders are systems thinkers—not local cause-and-effect thinkers.

If a spouse changes in some significant way, the other spouse now has a problem. This problem could jeopardize the organization called "marriage." If you have one incompetent person in any system, the system is compromised—it will not work as intended.

THE COMPETENT ORGANIZATION

Changes in systems—that is, the processes of which the systems are comprised— have to be both possible and to the benefit of the overall system.

That is part of the competent leader's role.

Task 2: People-making—making extraordinary people out of ordinary people

Most people are just that—ordinary people. If you're trying to staff your organization with extraordinary people, you won't be able to do it. There are not nearly enough of those to go around.

So you have to transform them from ordinary to extraordinary—from relatively incompetent to measurably competent. That's the hallmark of great organizations.

In WWII, Patton did not have competent people delivered to him. What he had were draftees. They didn't even want to be there. So he had to start from less than scratch.

In briefest form, what he did was this:

- He made choices about his own staff. He chose the ones he considered to be "make-able."
- They had to be the most competent people available in the specific roles they were to fulfill.
- Beyond that, they had to be disciples—even evangelists—about his aims and methods.
- They had to believe in the way he believed. He gave them no option.
- His mission had to be their mission. He gave them no option.

And *then*, those on his staff had to replicate what he did with them with their own staffs or their own soldiers. And so on, down to the corporals.

He was tough—on himself no less than on others. He was demanding—of himself no less than of others. He was loved by his troops. They knew he cared enough to refuse to let them default themselves—the most powerful form of **caring** there is. He was as advertised: "Let's get where we're going. Let's do what we have to do. So we can get back home."

He demanded competence. Not obedience, but competence. He expected the same of all of his other officers and noncoms. He was not a "Yes" man. He wanted no "Yes" men in his army. He didn't demand excellence. He demanded only full competence. And he was capable of teaching the lowest ranks how to be competent as individuals and as members of a team.

His Third Army had the lowest attrition rate and the highest retention rate in all of the Allied forces, even though they typically led the charge.

There is something indispensable about **competence**.

There is only one way to make extraordinary people out of ordinary people. And that is to relentlessly make it necessary for them to get better everyday at what they do in the organization.

The famous Admiral Lord Nelson did much the same. He made competent believers and performers out of his ship's captains, and then set them free to win the battle of Trafalgar by whatever means they could imagine. He knew that they had made every one of their ship's personnel daily more competent at what they did. They could then improvise as the occasion demanded. It was that improvisation that won the battle.

There are two other lessons from the history of great organizations that will be to your benefit:

- No matter what small part of the organization (or in total) you own, never take on a person who is not in the learning mode. You can't make performers out of people who are not capable of being "made" into competent performers. Don't take them on board. If it does happen, lighten the load by eliminating them—the sooner the better. As Yoda said, "There is no 'Try.' There is only 'DO.'"

- There is this matter of "*casting*." We forget that there are two aspects of this: those doing the casting and the person being "cast" in some role. Make the person own the problem. It is after all his (or her) career or even life that is at stake. The leader's role? Don't let the candidate make a mistake.

Most people are miscast. Certainly all people are miscast when they take on a new role, especially CEOs. They have to *learn* how to perform the role at least competently, if not masterfully. If they are not capable of learning how, trying to "develop" them is a waste of time and money.

Leaders do not permit themselves to be cast in a role they are incapable of learning how to master. "Know thyself."

Leaders do not cast others in a role they are incapable of learning how to master. If those others are in the learning mode, it may be possible. If they are not, it is most likely impossible.

If you're in the people-making business, as leaders are, you have to learn how to "make" others by first "making" yourself. Who would you have to be in order to perform those two roles masterfully?

Task 3: Becoming the provider and orchestrator of *meanings* in your organization

We have had a skirmish with this most profound of subjects previously.

There is no *meaning* in the universe. All meaning comes from people explaining things.

There is no meaning *in* a person observed. There is no meaning *in* his or her actions. There is no meaning *in* things or events or happenings.

Whatever something means is what people say it means. This is as true for scientists as it is for poets. It is a potential bugbear for all leadership. Unless the meaning of some happening propels the organization in its chosen direction, it will propel the organization in some other direction.

That is why becoming the looked-to source or orchestrator of meanings is such a basic task of leadership.

Even more than the other two, this is a basic task which has to be continuous. It has to be begun. But it can never be concluded. It will get somewhat easier, because those around you will be infected. They will do what you do—create or orchestrate the meanings of things that propel the organization in its chosen direction.

You have to be constantly listening to the music of the meanings of things that swirl within and around the organization. You have to intervene when necessary to impose the meanings of things that you need.

This is more than just "spin." You have to consider thoroughly how things have to be explained in a way that is advantageous to the mission of the organization. Otherwise you will get conventional meanings. And these will lead you ineluctably to conventional outcomes.

For example, a "problem" is never an obstacle. It is an opportunity to learn and grow in competence. Say so.

What is going on in the world is relevant only if you can make it mean something critical to the future of your organization.

Gossip has to be reinterpreted so that it means something of value to the performance of the organization, or to any of its people.

Irrelevancies have to be shot down whenever and wherever they occur, regardless of who offers them.

You must make it necessary for people to tell you what you *need to know* to perform your role better, or what the organization needs to know to better perform—not what those people happen to know. You must make it necessary for your key players to do the same thing.

Meanings are often implicit. Premises are rarely revealed. This is what you need to attack. "You know what I mean" won't do. People must say what they mean and mean what they say. That will provide you with the clues you need to uncover meanings—and thus to displace those meanings with better ones to advantage the organization.

"Why did so-and-so happen?" The meaning you attach to it doesn't have to be "true." It has to be much more than that. It has to do the work of propelling the organization in its chosen direction.

The advantage or the disadvantage will always lie in what things are said to mean.

Everything people want to talk about or deal with has to be interpreted. It is a matter of providing yourself and others with the interpretations the organization needs to fulfill its mission.

As the chief steward of the organization's mission, you have to endorse the interpretations that do the right kind of work. Or displace them with an interpretation that has a more propelling, compelling meaning.

Role descriptions, including yours, have to be created to set forth the meanings of things to be lived by. Meanings get created or changed in everyday conversations. Be there—in your own or others'.

That's where the music of meanings is played. Make that music right, or suffer the consequences.

If you learn how to perform these three tasks masterfully, you will perhaps slowly, but you will surely, produce a sustainably competent organization.

PART III

Refer back to the infrastructure for understanding competent organizations provided in the previous pages as you wish—or as you may need to.

It will always be the case: *as you think, so shall you do.* The "doing" part is never any better than the "thinking" part. No tool—including these conceptual tools—is ever any better than the understanding of the person who uses them.

Superior understanding offers two indispensable advantages:

1. It provides you with a far better "handle" on *what* to do; and

2. It provides you with the *why* it should be done one way rather than another.

Everyone can implement the ideas that they have in their minds. But implementing a wrong idea will lead you astray.

Implementing it in the wrong way is even more disadvantageous. You can correct a bad idea. No one sees that. But you cannot as easily correct a bad action. The consequences of that will linger on. You will lose credibility.

So the infrastructure we have laid in place in the preceding pages is of vital importance to you, because it is vital to your understanding of "What?" you could or should do, and "Why?" you should do it one way rather than another.

The best tool in the wrong hands will not accomplish what was intended.

In this part of the book, we will delve into the "Core Stratagems."
The better you get these down, the better strategist you will be about the
"What?" and the "Why?"

10. The Core Stratagems

All strategies for doing anything whatsoever are derivatives of a master strategy. One of these is who you ARE. Another is what you are trying to ACCOMPLISH in the longest term. That is, what are you *for?* What do you intend to **become** in your lifetime? What is the *cause* that you belong to—that you use for guidance day after day?

Small purposes must serve the interests of larger purposes. If you have no purposes beyond yourself, you will be adrift in the tides of time and happenstance.

Your purpose in something as small as an ad hoc conversation will depend upon your purpose for your life. If you do not have one, your conversation will turn on the pushes and pulls of the moment.

Your core stratagems (such as these) should be deeply embedded in your psyche—in your mind and in your heart. They must reveal who you are and what you stand for. They are the means of manifesting who you are and what your reason for existence is.

You must always *be up to* something. It makes little difference whether or not others know what you are up to, as Patton said. But it makes a great deal of difference whether or not you know what you're up to, and why.

If you don't strategize the small things, you cannot reach beyond them.

*Being *Had By* a Cause*

The first of these core stratagems which should not be skipped is that of being **had by** your cause.

If you "have" a cause, that will have some appeal. But if you are had BY your cause, you become relatively irresistible.

Part of the reason is that if you are had BY your cause, you will have to see it through. You can't simply abandon it like people who "have" a cause. So you are more compelling because people see you are in it for life—no matter what.

If you look back at the great leaders over all of human history, you will see that they were HAD BY the cause they espoused and struggled to fulfill. They were not dilettantes just talking a good story. They had no choice but to fulfill their cause. This meant, if you joined them, you had no options. You were HAD BY their cause.

The question that is most often asked is this:

> *"But suppose I don't feel HAD by my cause. I simply want to appear to have a 'mission.' Won't that work?"*

There are two answers to that:

- It might work with a few people some of the time. But if they perceive you are not held by the skin and the hair by your cause, they will be as lukewarm about it as you are. They stand ready to abandon you at any time. They won't be "loyal" to a person who hasn't staked his or her life on their cause.

- The other answer is this: If you *perform* being HAD BY your cause until you believe it yourself and others are totally won over by your performance, that will work. Others interpret your inner life by how you perform your values and beliefs. They have no direct access to your inner life.

The key point here is that leadership is a performing art. It's how you perform your role in the eyes of others that matters.

Still, as Lincoln said, you cannot fool all of the people all of the time. It takes a great performance on your part to convince people—either way—of your life or death determination to fulfill your cause. It is your performance that compels and impels them.

People live by their interpretations. They do no live by the facts. If we did, we would have no need for words or for communication. We would all be driven by the "facts."

It is in the interpretations people impose that leadership lives. And this simply requires a great performance on your part. That performance begins with being HAD BY your cause. Whether you *are* or merely auditioning as being HAD BY your cause, it depends upon how convincingly you perform it.

Admittedly this may not be entirely palatable to those amongst us who assume that we can be literal—that we need no interpretations.

But great actors on the stage or screen get paid nicely for their convincing performances. When you are talking to your peers or subordinates, you might imagine you are being paid for dealing only with "the facts." You should not be. You are being paid for performing a role at a convincing level. If you are not convincing in that role, you should perhaps consider some other role in life.

But of course any other role requires your convincing performance.

That leadership is a performing art is inescapable. Churchill himself stated as much. Alexander the Great knew he was playing a role on a huge stage. Without publicity and what we would today call "buzz," what would Gandhi have achieved?

Leadership is a role. You weren't born knowing how to perform it. How much impact you might have in that role depends upon how convincingly to other people you perform it.

People who perform *themselves* in that role are always second-rate, at best. It isn't "authenticity" (whatever that is) that seduces other people. It is your performance in that role. Ask any courtesan, prince, or politician.

No matter how you come by it, people—especially your disciples—must be deeply convinced that you are HAD BY your cause.

That is the sine qua non for all of the other stratagems. You cannot make them fully effective unless you start there.

*Strategically Distributing the *Ownership* of Problems*

[A discussion of these stratagems has appeared elsewhere in my writings—most notably in my book *Leadership: Thinking, Being, Doing.*]

Getting the right people to **own** just the right problems is critical. Most organizations do this poorly. Competent organizations do it well.

Competent organizations do this consciously and purposefully. They *strategically distribute* the ownership of every problem that might bear upon the performance of the organization.

- The least obvious may be the fact that more and more people these days don't know what they want to be when they grow up—so they don't (grow up, that is). If they take a job in your organization (shame on you!), they expect you to make them happy and cater to their real or imagined needs. If you have lots of these retarded adults in your organization, it will function much like an adult day-care center.

- If you can't make responsible adults out of these people, you will be stuck with respect to making a competent organization. If they cannot make competent people out of themselves, they will be intractably unable to make a contribution to making a competent organization.

- Still, the only way out of this predicament is to make it *necessary* for them to **own** the problems of their present performance and their future in this world.

- That's one example of what is meant by distributing the **ownership** of problems to those who *ought to* own them.

There are many other examples that can be used to shed light on this fundamental stratagem:

- If a person creates a problem as a result of incompetence or inattention, he or she **owns** that problem and its consequences and must take responsibility for fixing it.
- If a person creates a problem as a result of incompetence or inattention (or lack of engagement) for others in the organization, that person must take the lead in resolving the problem and dealing with the consequences.
- Every person who is engaged in a "moment of truth" (as Carlzon labeled it) *is* the company and must perform competently as the steward of the organization's mission. They **own** the problems of their performance and its consequences.
- Whoever sees or anticipates a problem **owns** the problem of getting the problem before the attention of the people who *should* own it and actively participating in its resolution.
- Every person **owns** the problem of not bringing their own problems into the organization. They get paid for performing, not for having problems that interfere seriously with their own or others' performance.
- Every member of the organization **owns** the problem of how to contribute to the elevated performance of all others around them.
- Every person in any work group or system **owns** the problems of bringing in the right people for the right roles, of integrating that person into the (competent) culture of the organization, and of evaluating that person's performance in order to make that person daily more competent.
- Every person **owns** the process of enhancing the organization's image and reputation.
- Every person **owns** his or her own learning and development, as well as the process of involving others (who can help) in that process.
- Every person **owns** the problem—the *moral* obligation of furthering the health and welfare of the whole organization, and of improving upon *its* performance daily.

Who should be involved in inventing better products, better services, better ways of doing things? **Everyone** should be.

THE COMPETENT ORGANIZATION

There are others. But you get the point. Strategically distributing the ownership of problems to those who *ought* to own them is indispensable to the development of a competent organization.

This turns conventional thinking upside-down. From a distant perspective, our conventional organizations look like a place where the employees create problems and managers are there to solve them. This way of doing things is not only extremely costly. It is stupid.

So don't consider this way of thinking as merely an ideal. This way of thinking is necessary if you are to have a fully competent and sustainably competent organization.

We have pandered to those who can't—or mostly *won't*. No one wins in this way of doing things. Get the ownership of problems rightly distributed and everyone wins. Well, maybe not the managers.

Because in a competent organization, you simply don't need the layers and layers of managers ("bad cops") to ensure that things get done in spite of the incompetence of those doing the work.

What you get if you do it in the conventional way is incompetent managers directing and controlling (etc.) what are assumed to be less-than-competent people doing the work.

This kind of thinking is not idealistic. It is realistic. It is the practical solution to what is otherwise an intractable problem.

The actual organization is not the one represented by the "org chart." The actual organization evolves from *who* owns *what* problem. Decentralization means getting the organization's daily problems owned by those closest to where the problems occur.

If "the boss" owns the problems of the subordinate's performance, there are two consequences:

- The subordinate *can't* then own the problems of her own performance; and

- Now we have two people engaged in talking about performance. It isn't the talk that accomplishes things.

The problems that people don't **own** will be problems they feel no responsibility for.

The more sense people have of **owning** the local and therefore vital problems of the organization, the more tied they will be to the life and the destiny of the organization.

*Make Possible What's Necessary . . . *

It is a basic task of leadership to make possible what is necessary—that is, what has to be accomplished.

There are two major reasons for this:

- One is that it doesn't make sense to cast people in roles that they are not fully competent to perform, even though this is done routinely in conventional organizations.

- The other is that if people are embedded in "dumb" systems, they cannot perform at the level required or expected.

The **first** is about casting people in roles. Too often, we think in terms of either credentials or of "potential." Both are slippery.

Credentials—no matter how positively spun they may be—are never any guarantee of future performance. Neither is "experience," as we have seen. Getting marks in school is about education. It is not about learning. If the person is not irreversibly in the learning mode, be actively skeptical—because that is what people are *supposed* to learn at university: how to learn.

Being impressed by the person's "potential" is another trap. A potential exists when it has been demonstrated. Otherwise, it is wishful thinking (on your part or that person's part).

We've talked about "casting." It is the candidate's responsibility to get himself or herself cast in the right role. Usually, they will defer to you. You can't know what they are *really* up to, or what their intellectual limits may be, or even their physical limits. You can't know what level of commitment they are capable of making. You can't know how competent they are until that has been tested.

If you can't do that in the recruiting and interviewing stages, ask them to consider a provisional term of employment. Competent people won't be offended by that. In fact, they will welcome the challenges you put before them. Incompetent people will be offended. There's your clue.

Once in the role, if they can't or don't accomplish what they have agreed to, consider it a default arrangement. Be done with it.

The **second** is about having in place "dumb" systems that limit or constrain top performance. If you have competent people, they will identify these for you, or change them into "smart" systems on their own.

If they are incompetent people, they will blame the "dumb" system but do nothing about it. Incompetent people flourish in "dumb" systems. If you let this happen, you have not composed the organization as you should have.

Make it necessary for people to work in "smart" systems—those that are demanding but channel performance in the right direction. Then you can readily identify incompetent people. They won't be able to perform in even the smartest systems.

If you are the chief executive, you are the only one who can make "smart" systems out of "dumb" systems. In any event, you are the only one who can endorse such changes. Make certain they are not devised for incompetent people, but for competent people. If you don't, you will already have shot yourself in the foot: **you** are the problem.

Make it necessary for every person routinely to become more competent. Make it necessary for every system to serve the best interest and needs of competent people. If you don't, everything will regress to the mean—the average.

* . . . and Make Necessary What's Possible*

The first part is relatively easy. This part is far more challenging.

You don't know what's possible. People say they know. But you can't know until it has been demonstrated. And even then, there is probably a way of accomplishing what has to be accomplished.

> When I was in high school, I suffered a severe "Charlie horse" in my right quadriceps playing sandlot basketball.
> My father, a great disciplinarian, had never driven me to the school—some 10-12 blocks away.
> But I went to him anyway that next morning and asked him if he would give me a ride to school. "What's the matter? You can't walk?"
> "No, sir," I said. "I can't. I got a terrible Charlie horse playing sandlot basketball yesterday and I can't walk."
> "Show me how you can't walk," he said.
> I did. I couldn't walk forward. I had to drag my right leg behind me.
> I demonstrated the slowness by which I had to move.
> "I see," he said. "Then start earlier."

It was not *necessary* that he drive me to school. It was *possible* for me to get there on my own. Just not in the habitual way.

What's *possible* may often require non-conventional thinking—as we might say "thinking outside the box."

We are all trapped in our "boxes." We think in ruts, and we carry out our daily tasks from our well-worn routines. What's possible may lie outside of the "ruts" we usually go down.

So the leader's purpose in making what's possible *necessary* is to shake people out of their lethargies. It is to spur some imagination about what might be possible if one were not constrained by previous thinking or experience.

It is this kind of growth of competence that competent organizations nurture. Doing something "better" may indeed require us to conceive of a better *way* of doing that something.

Those who are less than fully competent in their roles are constrained by their habitual ways of thinking and doing. A challenging accomplishment is not important enough to them to put more effort into it. So they just say "It just wasn't possible," pick up their paycheck anyway, and go home. Or maybe they have become ossified at thinking only "inside" the box.

Two observations here:

- One is that conventional organizations often pay incompetent people the same as competent people. They don't want to "discriminate." So the incompetent people get protected and the competent people have to carry the load—or leave.

- The other is that their superiors often accept the story that "It just wasn't possible." That's because they are no better at thinking about some alternative to a fixed mental model. They typically don't think about accomplishment whatever it takes, but about the well-worn paths they have always taken.

Competent people are not only competent at what they do. They are also competent at inventing a way to make possible the "impossible."

Competent leaders enlist competent people by pushing and pulling for a way to accomplish something that is said to be "impossible."

Competent organizations raise the bar and smash the boundaries of what is possible. They know that what is deemed "impossible" is most often a failure of imagination. Or of the wherewithal necessary to carry out a different way of proceeding.

*Leaders have to make **possible** what is necessary to be accomplished, and at the same time to make **necessary** what is possible.*

Competent organizations invent a way forward where there is not a familiar or readily obvious one.

LEE THAYER

Accomplishments, Not Activities

From top to bottom and side to side, competent organizations are accomplishment-minded.

The typical "job description," as we have seen, is a list of activities required of the "job," and a list of qualifications for the "job."

Qualifications are easily faked. And most employees are capable of carrying out the requisite *activities*. Their arguments at their yearly evaluation meeting are that they carried out those activities. Little or nothing was said about attitude, growth in competence, or accomplishments.

In a marginally incompetent organization, "jobs" are portrayed as the activities required. So people in such organizations are activity-minded, not accomplishment-minded.

"I did my job, didn't I?!" is the usual retort if an evaluation in negative. The evaluator often assumes that there should be something accomplished. But that is not on the "job description." They also often assume that the person *should* be getting better at what they do. But that is also not on the "job description."

Competent organizations do not have "job descriptions." They have "Role Descriptions." Those have three parts.

The first part is a description of what a virtuoso in that role would become capable of accomplishing even under adversity. It is not a description of what any incumbent is presently capable of *doing*. It is a description of what would be expected of that person over time.

The second part is essentially a contract that sets forth "Performance Goals" for the present and the mid-term. A performance goal is an objectively measurable accomplishment on a time-line. The person and his or her leader discuss these and agree both on the measurement and on the timing.

The third part of a Role Description is a Learning Plan. The person and his or her "boss" discuss the person's shortfalls in the role, and develop a measurable plan for eliminating them. They may be skills, attitudes, or mental shortcomings.

You can't just request that people be accomplishment-minded. You have to make it necessary.

These are tools for making accomplishment-mindedness *necessary*.

Don't hire people for key roles unless they have been accomplishment-minded in their own lives. Don't ask them if they were, or are. Such literal questions will enmesh you in their spin.

Ask them questions like this:

> *What have you learned from your past experience that turned out to be false?*
>
> *When you assess other people, how do you discriminate between mediocre people and real achievers?*
>
> *In your reading, do you go after success stories or stories of mistakes and failure?*
>
> *What kind of "boss" do you need?*
>
> *What is your primary interest in other people, and what do you do about it?*

What you're after in the first question is whether or not the person is in the Learning Mode. People learn primarily from their mistakes, not their successes.

Second question: Their answers will tell you whether *they* are mediocre or not. Achievers are outsiders. They are not appreciated. How has this person handled *that*?

Third question: If they don't know that, they don't know much of anything relevant.

LEE THAYER

If they are after the improved performance of other people, they are accomplishment-minded. It contributes nothing to complain about others' shortfalls. The question is, what did they do about that?

The most revealing of all: If they are talking to you because they are trying to accomplish something worthwhile in their own lives, they may be viable candidates. In other words, if they know what they want to be when they grow up, they will already be on the path.

If they want to be on *your* path, they are more likely to be just sycophants. If they choose your organization and you because it serves *their* best long-term interests, you have something more to learn from them.

People who are in the Learning Mode are always valuable to those who are in the learning mode. If you are, you can trust your intuition. Try to learn from them. If you can't, they probably don't belong with you.

On the other hand, *if you are not fiercely accomplishment-minded,* you will choose people who themselves are not. If you are, you will choose people who are more accomplishment-minded than you are.

When people report to you, don't ask them what they "did." Make it necessary for them to tell you only what they *accomplished*. It won't work perfectly at the outset. But it will underwrite your expectations about being accomplishment-minded in the long term.

Everything is about accomplishment. If you don't have that orientation, you are not going to have a competent organization.

Of course people always have "reasons" why they didn't accomplish what they promised (to themselves or to you). Unless those reasons are that they had something more important to accomplish, they are likely just excuses . . .

To be continued . . .

11. More on the Core Stratagems

Accomplishments, Not Activities

. . . We are picking up where we left off in the last chapter, exploring how much of our culture encourages lives of activities and not of accomplishments.

That may be true of the larger culture. But if you let it be true of your organization's culture, you can abandon any hope of ever having a competent organization. Being accomplishment-minded is simply a prerequisite to full competence in any role—for individuals and for organizations.

You will remember my story about my father and my walking problem. He was trying to teach me about the difference between accomplishments and activities. He wanted me to learn that they are two entirely different things. Getting a ride to school would have been merely an activity on my part, like a jacket that could be put on or taken off.

In our culture, we raise children and train them to engage in "activities." If they bake a cake, they use a recipe. They feel that if they follow the recipe, they have dispatched their obligations. If the consequences don't turn out as they should, it is not their fault.

Accomplishments are about the consequences of what is done. Activities are merely the method. For years in organizations, there were what were called "Policies and Procedures." They told you what to do. The accomplishment was somehow assumed. The accomplishment should never be assumed. It is the reason for doing what is done.

Activities are merely the means to some desired end. What needs measuring is not the activities, but the accomplishment.

People continually make promises to themselves and to others. They may be implicit. But they are still promises. In our culture, people are immersed in "relativism." The circumstances take precedence over the promises. If it is inconvenient or too difficult to keep one's promises, it is the promises that are not kept. The culprit is excused by his or her excuses.

This demoralizes the person as well as the person who buys the excuses wholesale. Character comes from making no promises you will not keep.

It is impossible to make a competent organization out of people who routinely lie and deceive one another.

Relationships

Everything is done out of some sort of relationship. If you run from a bear, it is your imagined relationship with that bear that propels your aversion.

We become who we are in our human and social relationships. Who we **are** is a product of our past, present, and imagined relationships.

Relationships enable and constrain what we do—as well as why and how we do what we do. They are fundamental. They are inescapable. Where there is no experienced relationship, nothing can be done. When there is, the nature of the relationship determines what can be said, what can be done, and how.

People don't even touch one another unless there is a relationship that permits that.

Consistent with our cultural norms, you might imagine that what is done makes possible a relationship. It certainly looks that way. But it is the opposite: the relationship determines what is possible.

For those in leadership positions, it is the relationship they have with their people that enables what is possible, and what may be necessary. The relationship precedes. The relationship you have with others and they with you both enables and constrains what is possible.

Leaders first create the relationship they need with themselves for fulfilling their role. Then they must create the relationships they need with others in order to fulfill the mission of the organization.

Competent organizations are built on relationships. If the right relationship exists, you can improvise. If it doesn't, you are stuck with more or less explicit routines and procedures.

For example, those who work in call centers work from a handbook that tells them what to say. There was a cartoon in the *New Yorker* years ago that pictured a man and a woman reading in bed beside one another. Both were reading sex manuals. Nothing else was happening. That had to suit the relationship or it wouldn't be done.

"Branding" is a fairly contemporary "marketing" attempt at creating a relationship between a company's products and its customers. Yet, if every headache remedy is advertised as better than every other headache remedy, which do you buy? You trust *your* brand.

The Marines build lateral relationships. It is the dogface next to you who might determine whether you live or die. That's a "band of brothers" kind of relationship.

Relationships are ubiquitous because nothing happens if they don't exist.

Here's a way of making this felt, but intangible, condition of being in a relationship more comprehensible:

- What kind of relationship do leaders need with themselves?
- What kind of relationships do leaders need between themselves and their people?
- What kind of relationships do leaders need between themselves and their other constituents, and between them and their stakeholders?

- What kind of relationships do people need in organizations between themselves and their superiors, their subordinates, and their peers and colleagues?
- What kind of relationship do leaders and their people need between them and who they would have to be to have a fully competent organization?

There are no recipes because people are different, circumstances are different, and aims are different. But competent organizations forge the kind of relationships they need *in order to* make daily progress on their cause, their aims. They create the kinds of relationships needed to facilitate their collective movement in the right direction.

The relationships are conceived and invented as subordinate to the aims of the organization. When relationships are not **subordinated** *to the aims of the organization, they become impediments to those aims.*

The possibilities and consequences of relationships extends from the most casual two-person conversation to meetings within and outside the organization to the public image of your organization. It is the nature of the relationship that underwrites what can and cannot be done, what will and will not be done.

You cannot harbor expectations that lie outside what is possible in the relationship. For salespeople and retail clerks and "customer service" people, what can and cannot be accomplished is given by the relationship.

What it comes down to is this:

> *It takes competent people to make a facilitating relationship* ***if*** *and when they are guided by a collaborative accomplishment.*
>
> *It takes facilitating relationships to make a competent organization.*
>
> *It takes a competent organization to achieve a chosen destiny and legacy.*
>
> *The relationships you cannot create produce a destiny you cannot have.*

Choice

This is an intriguing one. But it is a potent one. Once you see it work, you will rarely if ever let it go.

In principle, it is quite simple:

- If you are a leader, you must assume that everything about people and their performance is by **choice**.
- They may try to attribute their successes to themselves and their shortfalls to other factors. Don't buy it.
- The crux of the matter is this: No one can stand in front of you and choose to be other than who they are or how they are capable of performing at that moment.
- The same is true for you standing before a mirror.
- Who we are and what we are capable of is a consequence of the accumulated choices we have made in the past.
- Who we will be and what we will be capable of in the future is a consequence of the choices we made yesterday and today, and the choices we will make tomorrow.

So everything about who people **are** and what they are capable of IS by choice. It's just that the effects are cumulative—from the past and into the future.

Let us now add three:

- People may make choices. But how things actually turn out will depend upon a host of other—largely random or serendipitous—factors.
- The choice-maker does not control the outcomes. So what we are talking about here is making choices with uncertain outcomes.
- If you don't choose, you lose. You will simply be a victim. If you do choose for a rightful outcome, you may not win. But you will grow in stature and in the capacity to choose wisely and well. That's the best you can do.

People may refrain from choosing on the grounds that they can't control the outcomes. They prefer being the victims of what comes their way, and they may vote for those who will "protect" them from their failure to choose their own path.

Reality—what happens on your way to your future—will always play a role. Sometimes a decisive role.

People can't really choose the final outcomes of their choices. But they become better people for making them and doing whatever it takes to fulfill—by becoming more competent—their choices. So they win either way.

It is undeniable that people cannot choose who they will be or what they will be capable of today. They've already made those choices.

And it is undeniable that organizations cannot choose what they will become and what they will be capable of. But the payoff lies in what they choose and how diligently they go about vindicating their choices. That's a gain that can be had only by those who live by *choice*.

And that's why competent organizations live by choice. They want to take both the credit and the blame.

> *"Choice" is a core stratagem because it is the source of the organization's determination and resiliency.*

The Learning Mode

In a competent organization, people are selected because they are in the "learning mode." Those in the learning mode may not be better. But they will over a short period of time surpass those who were better at the time of induction.

It is a core stratagem of leadership to make it **necessary** for everyone in the organization who might be the source of a "moment of truth" to be in the *learning mode.*

Real learning is the source of real change for the better. Change prescribed by the power players may or may not be for the better. It is only when it is a way of life for most people in the organization that you can have a fully competent organization.

Here I'm going to paraphrase what appears on page 326 of my book *Leadership: Thinking, Being, Doing*:

- It makes no difference what the role is. Performance in that role can be improved upon every day . . . forever. Only those who are in the learning mode can do this.
- You don't have to preach "continuous improvement." People in the earning mode will improve upon their own performance and the procedures involved—without thinking about it.
- If they are not in the learning mode, make it **necessary** to be so.
- The learning mode is open-minded. The knowing mode is closed-minded.
- Learning requires questioning. Knowing leads to statements. The best performance always derives from the best questions.

Only people who are in the learning mode can be fully engaged in what they are doing. Others go through the motions by rote.

Where competence is at stake, there is no substitute for the learning mode.

Most of what we learn we have to learn by doing it, as Aristotle said many years ago. Only those who are in the learning mode can learn how to do something differently. All others are stuck in the repetitive gear.

They are not curious. They are not imaginative. They are not inventive. They already "know" how to do whatever they do. *Better* is not a concept of much importance to them.

So you can see where getting better all the time comes from. And getting better and better at what is done is a condition of the competent organization.

> For the competent organization, being in the **learning** mode is merely a prerequisite.

Life at Work

If you look at the most competent organizations, you will see that the people in them are more fully alive. Not in the "Ha! Ha!" sense. But in the sense that they are more alert, they are more engaged, and they are enjoying more what they are accomplishing.

As we have observed previously, it is only competent people who are more fully alive, happier in their work. *That's solely because they are good at it and always getting better.*

It is the relatively incompetent and/or aimless people who get depressed, stressed, and despondent. They are up against an adversary in life that they seem unable to name. That is because it is in *them.*

Wherever they go, they take the problem with them. There are pills for it. But competence beats pills anytime.

Competent people get themselves rightly cast, as we have seen. They enjoy their work. They enjoy helping others become more competent so they can enjoy *their* work.

Spiritually, they know that good work, well done, is a form of prayer. This is not a religious issue. It is a practical matter. People who love good work, and who are fully competent at it, are healthier both physically and mentally. They can afford to be humble. They are outgoing. They live longer.

And they live better lives because they love life as a result. They are adults, more fully human.

It is a core stratagem of leadership to nurture people, to bring them to full stature, to give them the best reason for being, to give them what they can get no other way.

What great leaders give people—because they demand it of people—is competence and purpose.

Great leaders throughout history have considered a job well done when they achieve a win-win: when their organization has fulfilled its mission, and when the people involved have become better human beings.

The two are really one. They are interconnected. It takes competent people to staff a competent organization. And it takes a competent organization to require more competence of its people. You cannot have the one without the other.

That's the real challenge of leadership. The only known path is through increased and increasing competence. If you can't make that necessary, it won't happen.

Return on . . .

Every organization has a way of measuring its own effectiveness. For most organizations, that is usually calculated as a "Return on . . . ." That may be a return on investment (ROI), or a return on capital, or a return on sales, etc.

But there is typically no such measure for what individual members return on . . . the investment in them.

That is because we do not consider their pay as an investment in them. Competent organizations do. Competent organizations consider their employees' pay—including the CEO and his or her staff—as down payment on what they should be worth to the company in the years ahead.

If someone's pay is $50,000 a year, that is a prepayment for the value they should return to the organization five or ten years in the future. It is the organization's investment in them, and it is their obligation to provide a healthy return on that investment.

We measure the organization in some "return on . . ." way. But we don't measure people in a similar way. That is a mistake—as common as it is.

An organization, for example, may use a P&L statement. It is *possible* to create P&L statements for individuals, for teams, and for departments.

That puts people in the same game the organization is in, as Jack Stack has suggested in *The Great Game of Business.*

The closer you can measure individual performance in the same way you measure organizational performance, the better the performance of both.

Church organizations, military organizations, philanthropic organizations, and educational and performing arts organizations have differing ways of measuring their performance. No matter. The point is to bring those ways of measuring into the organization as deeply as you can. That brings the members of the organization out of an insular organization and into the real world.

If they can't play the game the organization plays—however its performance is measured, and however metaphorical that may be, there will be a split between what they think is important and what is actually important for the organization.

It's only when spouses are equal stewards of the *institution* that they measure themselves against the health and welfare of the institution rather than some other (perhaps less relevant) criterion.

Every member of every organization needs to function as a steward of that organization's health, wellbeing, and mission. To do this, they must have a way of measuring their own performance in terms analogous to the way the organization is measured.

> *What the members of an organization have to invest is their contribution to the organization's aims. Give them a way of measuring that. They need it, and it will serve the organization better than most of the conventional "returns on . . ." in use today.*

Teaching by Questioning

This is sometimes referred to as the "Socratic method." Whatever you call it, it is a way of teaching by engaging the learner's mind always to its limits. It is a way of teaching by insight. It is contrary to all forms of teaching by rote.

In a competent organization, everyone is both a learner and a teacher. Leaders are, especially, teachers. The best learn how to teach by indirection—in stories, by example, and most powerfully with questions.

The best teachers do not "teach." They **lead** *their learners to the insights they need to "understand." They do this best by asking just the right next provocative question.*

They do this to engage the learner fully in his or her own learning. In conventional methods of "teaching," the learner is usually just a bystander.

An important caveat about teaching/learning:

> The SUFI recognized that the critical aspects of this enterprise are the preparedness of the learner and the capabilities of the teacher.

In his book *Learning How to Learn*—an auspicious title—Idries Shah had this to say about learners:

"The fact is that you can learn only what you can be taught."

In other words, no matter the method, learners can learn only what they are capable of learning. Once people know what they believe they need to know to last the rest of their lives, their capacity for learning dwindles into little more than trivia.

Real learning involves real change. If people have closed minds (because they are in the "knowing mode"), there is not much they can be "taught." If people are incapable of making the internal or behavioral changes that are implicit in what they might learn, they become incapable of learning.

Mentoring is therefore not a straightforward activity. People vary greatly in their capacity for learning. What they can't learn, they won't learn. They have to be prepared to learn what is being taught.

On the teacher's side of the system, Shah cites the SUFI scholar Ibn Arabi as follows:

"People think that a teacher should display miracles and manifest illumination. But the requirement in the teacher is that he should possess all that the [learner] needs."

So, yes, teaching/learning goes on all the time in a competent organization. But it can be no more fruitful than the capacity to learn and the strategic capability to teach.

That's why *the best tool available to the learner is just the right question.* And the best tool available to the teacher is just *the right question.*

Constructive Opinions

It would be impossible for you to shut down people's opinions about everything under the sun—and their assumed "right" to express their opinions.

But wrongheaded opinions can deflect the organization down a wrong path. So what do you do?

You have to have a top-priority rule. That rule is:

You have every right to your opinions and judgments. But before you express them, make sure that they are constructive, that they further the needs and interests of the organization and do not impede them.

I have no intention of telling you what your opinions should be, in the same way that you have no prerogative to tell me what my opinions should be.

But expressing them when they might be contrary to the best interests of this organization's health and welfare is something in which we have a mutual and equal obligation to avoid.

If they are "constructive," if they would be helpful to this organization's cause or mission, by all means express them forcefully. If they are "destructive," if they would be harmful to our common cause, do not express them.

More than your experience, more than your intelligence or your credentials, it is your ability to discern which is which that measures your—or anyone's—value to this organization.

If you can't personally enforce it, don't express it.

[One last observation about learning and life:

Ultimately, our lives consist of our experiences in and of life.

*The more you learn, the more you **can** learn. The more competent you are, the more competent you can become.*

That is the real fabric of life. We live in and by the pace and the relevance of our learning.

Nothing contributes more to the person or to his human connections than his competence in his roles in life.

That is why real leaders make that both possible, and necessary, for membership in their organizations.]

PART IV

If it wasn't obvious in the preceding, let us make it explicit:

Competent teachers, like competent leaders, strive mightily to make themselves redundant, unnecessary.

*As suggested by Lao-tzu centuries ago, their work is completed when they are no longer necessary. They **capacitate** and **enable** their learners and their people, so that their learners and their people are no longer dependent on them. That requires good learners as well. It requires both.*

They make their learners and their people *competent.* Today, we might refer to what they do as making their people and their learners capable of sustaining themselves, or their organizations.

This is no parlor trick. There are no "secrets." Competent teachers provide their learners with what *they* need to function intelligently and autonomously. Competent leaders provide their people with what they need and their organizations with what they need, in order to function competently without them.

This is typically missing in the recipes served up by the business press. It is almost as if all of that leadership flood of the past two or three decades was intended to make leaders *in*dispensable, rather than dispensable. We're taking the latter view. It's the one that actually works.

In what follows, we will explore some of the tools and techniques for making sustainably competent organizations—the aim of this book.

One proviso: these are generalized accomplishments. Specific cases require specific adaptation or even invention. These are tools and techniques for what you need to accomplish. You may even have to *invent* the path required to get there.

But here are some basic—practical and workable—ideas for what you should do to create a sustainably competent organization.

If you took to heart all of the preceding chapters, they will make sense to you. If they don't, I'd suggest you go back and review some of the earlier pertinent pages.

12. Basic Tools and Techniques

The logical place to start is at the beginning. You have to begin with a thorough understanding of roles, of role descriptions, and of how to implement them.

From the smallest casual interaction with another person to the largest of public stages, people are always performing the "role" they imagine themselves to be in. For the most part, these roles are tacit, implicit in the situation.

No one is born knowing how to play any role. We all have to learn how to play our roles by playing them and observing others.

Our behavior is always guided—enabled and constrained—by our assumptions about the role we are expected to play, and our own expectations of ourselves in any role we find ourselves in.

How we assume our roles constitutes the blueprints for our thinking, our feelings, and our behavior. We think and feel and do according to the roles we are called upon to perform.

Obviously, some people are better than others at performing their roles. And, just as obviously, most people can get better at playing their roles if they work at doing so.

At the beginning of social life, most of what we learn about playing roles is a matter of trial-and-error. As we mature, we "hang out" with those people and in those places where we have familiar and comfortable roles.

We go from the "learning mode" to the "knowing mode." We let the roles we seem to play well determine for us who we will *be*, and with which others we will be who we are in those roles.

There is much more to be understood about this basic mechanism of human and social life. But the above brief will suffice here. What we need to understand mainly is that the roles we play in life are unwritten, tacit.

What is different about their application in the making of competent *organizations* is that they are made explicit. They are not for pushing us hither and thither, but for *pulling* us in the direction we ought to be going—given our role(s) in the organization, and given *its* purpose.

The Role of the Organization

The first role about which you need to be keenly concerned at the outset and forever after is *the role* of your *organization*.

Your organization has its role in the dynamic real world of customers, employees, stakeholders, competitors, markets, the larger economy and the global economy, etc.

The questions you need to be able to answer about the role of your organization are:

- What is my organization FOR in the real world; and
- What role should it play in current affairs and in the history of the business it is in?

Why does your organization exist—that is, what is it FOR? It will indeed have a history—from birth until death. It will have a destiny, whether you choose it or not. It will have its own trials and tribulations, its own problems, its successes and its failures. How it performs in the real world will determine its health and its fate, independent of your hopes and dreams.

The best handle you will ever have on its present and its future is the one you devise when you think through and write down its *role*. It needs a role description. And you are the only one who can provide it.

This doesn't guarantee anything. It merely provides you with a trajectory from here to there. You need it to keep on course, or to get back on course if you are carried off course for any reason.

It is the guidance system for your organization.

Do you intend for your organization to be the best in the business by some or by *any* measure? Say so.

Do you intend for your organization to be known for the pace of its growth or its return to stockholders or its public acclaim? Say so.

Do you intend for your organization to take on any adversity that comes your way, and overcome it. Say so.

Do you intend for your organization to be user-friendly, to be the most trusted, the most caring? Say so.

When the history of the business you are in is written, do you intend for your organization to be singled out as the leader, the innovator, the trail-blazer, the standard-bearer? Say so.

When the history of the world is written, do you intend for your organization to have a special place? Say so.

What is your organization supposed to *mean* to its members? To its critics and its fans? To the public at large? To its competitors? To the generations that come after you? Set it forth in words or images.

Do you intend for your organization to make the world a better place? Say so.

Do you intend for your organization to be the preferred organization for all of your many and different stakeholders, or for only certain stakeholders (customers, for example)? Say so.

This is not a vacuous exercise. This is not an ego trip. This is not something to be hung on the walls of your organization.

THE COMPETENT ORGANIZATION

Every ship has one captain and one navigator. The captain determines where the ship is to go, and the navigator provides the means of doing so. In an organization, the captain is the CEO. The navigator is not a person, but the role of the organization—along the lines of the above and a score of other questions that need answers.

The answers mark the course to be taken. Only one person—you, the one in charge—needs to know the ultimate destination. But it takes many eyes and many efforts to keep the ship on course.

You need to describe the role of your organization in sufficient detail for you to plot a course and keep it. You may change it at any time. But it is consistently maintaining your course that is at stake.

As the old saying goes,

> *"If you don't know where you're going, you're likely to end up someplace else."*

Most organizations do end up "someplace else." And it is in *that* place that their thorniest problems arise.

[Just a reminder: The Mother of all tools is how you think about what needs thinking about. No other tool will serve you optimally unless and until you continue to hone that one to its maximum.]

Role Descriptions in General

It will help to review what role descriptions *are for your* people and what they are supposed to do for them and for the organization.

The most effective role descriptions for roles in your organization have three parts. (The role description for your organization has only one. Your role provides the other two.) The three parts are:

- The first part describes what a virtuoso in that role would be able to accomplish—under adversity. There are no activities listed here.

There are only accomplishments—explicit or implicit. It is a word picture of the *ideal* performance that you would expect of an incumbent who had been in that role for a period of time (not specified).

A very generic example might be: *You will perform this role better than anyone before you has performed it, and you will become the exemplar for all of those who may follow you in this role.*

Every item you put on the list must be at least potentially measurable on whatever general timeline you agree to.

You draft it and the potential incumbent drafts it. Then you get together to discuss the meaning of the words and how the two of you would independently or together measure progress.

What's important is not the document. That is merely to testify to your mutual accord. What's important is what you and the incumbent/potential incumbent understand their role to be.

This part of the role description functions like a template for the incumbent's development in the direction of virtuosity in that role over the long term.

When you have fully collaborated on the terms and their implications for the path from here to there, the incumbent sets forth a rough plan for his or her development in the direction of becoming the ideal and exemplary incumbent.

When either of the two of you wants to discuss again one of the criteria of the profile, or to make changes, you meet again, gain accord again, and move forward.

It is how the incumbent sees and acts on his or her role every successive day that is crucial. The piece of paper merely sets forth what the two of you have agreed to.

There might be ten or twenty targets on this profile. It is best to use bullets and keep it to one page. It is always provisional. The two of you can change it at any time. It may be out of sight. But it should never be out of mind.

As the incumbent's mentor (and/or "boss"), you may want to ask questions at random (or for good reason) about the person's progress on a particular item on the profile.

- The second part of a good role description can be referred to as "Performance Goals":

This is where you (primarily) set forth the immediate and mid-term goals to be accomplished.

They must be clear and objectively measurable. "Objectively" here means that anyone could understand them and how performance will be measured.

You meet with the role incumbent to discuss every performance goal on the list, to make sure each is fully understood.

When the incumbent is satisfied that he or she understands the goals to be achieved, they get back to you in a few days with a workable plan for achieving each goal. If you are convinced after questioning that the plan will work (or if you have an alternate to suggest), then it is a matter of monitoring every critical step.

If such performance goals do not have "teeth" in them, you are both wasting time. What this means is that you both understand what the consequences of failing to accomplish them will be. You want no surprises when the due date comes. In order to insure this, you may have to ask about progress on each goal from time to time—or establish in advance regular reports.

Each performance goal is your opportunity to help the incumbent develop his or her competencies as their achievement unfolds.

- The third part of a well-done role description is a specific Learning Plan. It is derived from your discussions with the incumbent about his or her shortfalls.

Those observed shortfalls (and always be specific here) may be thinking skills, attitudes, necessary interpersonal skills, or communication skills. They may be failures to keep promises. They may be inadequate beliefs about one's capabilities. They may be a failure to plan the work, or to work the plan.

Whatever they are, they must be *owned* by the incumbent. What this means is that the incumbent has to own the process of eliminating the shortfalls and demonstrating that the problems have been solved.

This is not a matter of reading a book (an activity) or taking a course (an activity). It is accomplishing the elimination of one or more shortfalls that is the measure.

You may want to mentor and otherwise help the incumbent if asked. You may want to suggest places and people that might be helpful.

What you will want to see on the date set for the plan to be accomplished is that the incumbent can and has performed without this or that shortfall.

[You will find examples of different kinds of role descriptions in Appendix A.]

Why Should You Use Role Descriptions of this Sort?

As we touched upon previously, role descriptions of this sort, well carried out, are far superior to the more conventional "Job Descriptions."

In the first place, you don't want people to have "a job" at your place. You want them to have a critical *role* in contributing to the health and welfare—and the destiny—of your organization. The difference is the kind of difference that determines whether or not yours will become a *competent organization*.

Your organization is always a work in progress—always telling its life story. You want people to have a rightful and indispensable role in this.

The best way I have found for doing this is through the use of potent *Role Descriptions*.

Never make bureaucratic exercises of the Role Description process. The long-term payoff always germinates in the face-to-face and highly focused discussions that the "superior" and the "subordinate" have about them. The paperwork, as mentioned, is solely for the purpose of making a record of the accords reached. The real value is in those confrontations, not in the paperwork.

The accords are *promises*, not hopes or intentions on the part of either participant in those discussions.

The failure to execute, if it does not come as a surprise, may have mitigating circumstances. The failure to keep promises is a serious character disorder. Doing role descriptions with "teeth" in them will reveal rather quickly those disorders.

You have to take the incumbent's word for it. If he says he will accomplish what he has agreed to, you have to believe him. Keep your doubts to yourself. But let them determine how carefully you need to monitor the process.

Have faith, as W. C. Fields purportedly said, but "cut the cards."

Your purpose here is not to pass judgment. It is to help the role incumbent to grow in stature and competence. Be helpful. Just be careful not to get pulled into owning their problem. Once they walk out the door, they now own the problem of their performance.

Help them if they need help. But avoid owning the problems that only they should own.

You use role descriptions of this sort and in this way because you want to make a competent organization. This is just one of the key tools for doing so.

There are three good reasons for learning how to use Role Descriptions as this kind of tool:

- By doing it this way, you *pull* people into competence rather than trying to *push* them into competence;

- By using Role Descriptions in the right way, you do away with the need for those controversial "performance appraisals." Role Descriptions are a way of making performance transparent and continuous.

- Rightly handled, Role Descriptions (R/Ds) actually *preclude* many of the thorniest problems that conventional organizations seem to have to deal with in perpetuity.

13. More Tools and Techniques: II

Before moving on—and if they have not already occurred to you—here are some other invaluable uses for Role Descriptions:

- A good and comprehensive role description is the best navigational tool you could use for recruiting and for interviewing candidates for any key role. Use only the first part. You can offer parts two and three as an example. Since the first part of the R/D is essentially about the future, you would be discussing not past credentials and experience—but what really matters—commitment to a role in making the future. When you are both looking at the same R/D document, the chances of getting the right person cast in the right role are much greater.

  When all of the key role descriptions are made available online within the organization, people can have a much better idea of how their roles fit together. It makes possible communication and information systems deriving from a *need to know*. If a person provides others with what those others *need* to know to perform at a higher level in their roles, they will do the same for that person. It may take a while, but they can learn how to do this.

- Role descriptions are a bit like the plot, the characters, and the themes for a story. That is the story that the organizations tells by its performance in the real world. Assuming that you have set forth the right roles, and have cast the right people in those roles, how they play their parts of the story determines how the story turns out. Their performances determine the performance of the organization as a whole.

Using R/Ds in this way contributes to how the organization gains in competence. What people routinely say and do become a part of the organization's culture. How roles are performed according to role descriptions provides an excellent impeller of any organization's culture. And that kind of culture will in turn provide many of the needed pushes and pulls for increasing the competence of the organization.

- The unique culture of every organization has imbedded in it the "rules of the road." Here are the implicit *proscriptive* (don't do this or that) and *prescriptive* rules (do this or that, and do it in this way) for conduct in that organization. When increasing one's competence is a foundational prescription for everyone in the organization, the **necessity** for doing so becomes everyone's mantra. It is only competent people who will create such a culture. Incompetent people will create a jumble of opinions and beliefs, none of which will contribute to the mission of the organization.

- Probably the least obvious but the most potent value of good role descriptions is that their careful use reveals a key ingredient of organizational competence: that of the sheer reliability of the self-assessments required. People vary greatly in the accuracy of their self-assessments. Once revealed, they can improve them.

In other words, intelligent and accurate self-assessments strengthen the performance of the organization. It is the sheer competence of people to assess accurately what they are and are not capable of undertaking that leaders want and develop in their people. Incapacities can often be fixed. Self-deception cannot.

The Four Covenants

Do not attempt to raise up the performance of the organization as a whole via slogans or recipes. They don't work. You are better off to work at improving the organization's performance piece by piece.

There is no magic formula or fairy dust that you can sprinkle which will do it for you. It has to be done person by person, piece by piece.

Here is the best tool I know of for accomplishing that:

Imagine the traditional "pyramid." (This will work with any organization structure. It's simply easier to visualize using the pyramid structure.) Start at the top. Consider in this piece of the organization all of those who report to the CEO. The *four covenants* that need to be made integral to those relationships are as follows:

1. First covenant: each of those persons, in their separate roles, has to *commit to becoming the best there is (or ever was) in that role.* Basic to this covenant is that they measurably improve their performance in their role continuously . . . and forever.

This has to be necessary for them personally because of who they are. If not, that necessity has to be provided by the CEO (or the organization's potent culture). Necessity here means there are no options.

In this powerful way of thinking and doing, there can be only two reasons for any shortfall:

- Either those persons are not competent in their roles; or
- There is not enough personal or external necessity for the level of performance required.

If it is necessary for them to do so, they *can* raise their level of competence, and thus their performance. If the optimum level of necessity just doesn't work, it is time to cast someone else in that role.

If you want a strong chain, you can't have weak links. You can't make a competent organization out of less-than-competent people. The organization cannot perform above the level of its internal performers—except by "luck."

This covenant means that the subordinate enters into a "life or death"—stay or go—contract with the superior. Intention, hopes, or promises don't count for much in a competent organization. There, it is understood that the *only* measure of performance is performance.

Performance is a measure of the *results*, not the preliminaries.

2. The **second covenant** requires the commitment of those persons to learn how to provide compelling leadership to all of those with whom they have dealings—whether vertically or laterally.

They learn how to do this in the best way there is—by being the best followers there have ever been. This does not mean becoming "Yes"-people. It is not a matter of blindly following orders. It is a matter of becoming increasingly competent in their roles and of leading not from their position in the organization, but from their competence in their roles.

Great followers are the ones who become extremely competent at "when to lead, when to follow, and when to get out of the way." More than that:

They have learned implicitly that the path to their own success lies in making their "boss" successful—no matter what.

The "boss" may be a lousy leader. If so, there are but two realistic choices:

- One is to develop him or her into a superb leader; and
- The other is to find elsewhere the "boss" you should have chosen in the first place.

Simply complaining to yourself and/or others will earn the complainer the label of "loser." If a bad boss survives you, you will look like a crank.

That's usually the only reward you will get for being the complainer. There will always be those who are quick to agree with you—until they see their own success in the organization to come from siding with the "boss" and not with you.

The best course of action to follow is almost always that of making your own boss successful. That's what great followers do.

Consider General Lee in the Civil War and his next-in-command General Longstreet. Longstreet respectfully disagreed with Lee's strategy (preceding the battle of Little Round Top). Lee heard him out, asked if he was finished, and said, "We will do it my way, and I expect you to lead the charge."

Longstreet had his day in court. He expected to lead the charge either way. So he did. He was an example of a great follower.

And Lee was a great "boss." As a leader, it will sometimes turn out that you made a bad judgment. But if you are the leader, you are the one who has to make it. If you and your key staffers continue to disagree, you all lose.

Someone has to call the shots when the heat is on. There is always a possibility that you will call what turn out to be the wrong ones. But that's when *great* followers put everything they've got into making it turn out well even if you were wrong.

When the follower becomes the leader, he or she will also make what may turn out to be wrong judgments. That's precisely when the leader really needs competent—even great—followers.

As a leader, you want and need the judgment of your followers. But, as Colin Powell has said, it inevitably becomes time to stop talking and start doing. When that time comes, the path must be clear,

And that path must be set by the leader. Learning how to make the leader successful is how followers become better leaders.

3. The **third covenant** is this:

Each of those key persons must agree to become competent to function *at all times* as the **chief steward** of the organization's mission.

That may seem strange. How many "chief" stewards can you have? We conventionally assume that is the leader's task. It is. But it is also everyone else's task. The more *owners* of a mission you have, the more likely it will happen. In the special forces—like the Navy Seals—the last man standing still owns the outcome.

The more owners of the mission you have—the more chief stewards of that mission—the more likely it will be carried out.

Let's go back to the CEO's staff—that top piece of the organization. Each of the persons who reports to the CEO must own **100%** responsibility for the health and welfare—and the destiny—of that organization. Don't divide that responsibility by allowing people to own 20% of that responsibility.

Go for the multiplier. My Irish grandfather—the farmer—taught me that the best team of horses was the team in which every horse was trained to perform the task alone if necessary. The multiplier came from having, say, four such well-trained horses in harness. Together, that would give you far more than four "horsepower."

To have but one person who owns that responsibility, and who tries to manipulate the organization from that single fulcrum doesn't really make practical sense. It may be the conventional way of doing things. But it doesn't work nearly as well.

What does make sense of course is getting most of the members of the organization pulling it in the right direction. I know of no serious disagreement about this. But it's like the weather: everybody complains about it, but no one does anything about it. The popular business press hasn't been of much help. You can't fix what needs fixing at its core by sprinkling fairy dust over it.

Or by offering 15,000 varieties of pop psych remedies for the symptoms. It has to be righted at the core. The problem is not a "psychological" one. Fixing it begins with this covenant. This book offers actionable solutions to otherwise illogical problems.

You create a covenant that simply makes it necessary. The leader's role is not to be the only or even the main chief steward of the organization's health and welfare. The leader's role is to make it necessary for others to do the pushing and pulling. The wagon driver does not make the wagon go. He makes it necessary for the horses to make the wagon go—and in the right direction.

Do some simple math. If one person is pulling and another person is lagging, the person doing the pulling is struggling just to be half-effective.

How much "horsepower" the organization has depends both upon how much pulling and pushing is going on, and how much braking is provided by those who are not pushing and pulling.

Starting at the top piece, if each of the persons involved own 100% of the problem, you have powerful collaborative (and thus multiplied) energy and attention at work. Leave other options open, and many people will choose those.

If people are not there for the organization (for "Mother"), they will be there for other reasons. Those other reasons are often like dragging brakes. You are paying for forces that work against the mission of the organization.

There are always covenants of one sort or another at work. Make them the ones the organization needs. Surgeons talk about the "kindest cut." That's what this is. It benefits the organization which in turn benefits the people in it. And they also benefit directly from an orientation that derives from reality and not some fad or folklore.

Everyone needs to own the outcomes. Make it so.

4. The **fourth covenant** is that those on the CEO's staff have to commit themselves as follows:

- To perform their own roles better than they do—better tomorrow than today, and ever after.
- To become the best in their role there ever was—or ever will be (this reprises the first covenant).
- To perform a role like yours (the leader's) better than you do. The surest way of doing this is to learn how to make you more effective in *your* role. They learn how by helping you get better in your role.

In our culture, people are often upwardly mobile. At least they like to think this way. They are always looking up.

This is not good. There should be no corporate "ladder" to climb. People begin to imagine that they might be more competent if only they had a higher-level job.

Don't deceive them by encouraging their interests in being promoted. In a fully competent organization, it is the person who is most competent in his or her own role who deserves attention. Not the person who is always looking at the next step and therefore may be neglecting his or her present role.

If you promote from within on the basis of ambition rather than competence, you are likely to end up with a less-than-competent organization. In other words, a mediocre one.

You want people studying your *role* performed ideally, not studying *you*. It is in helping you see the discrepancy between how you perform and how you should be performing that they make their contribution. If they are merely ambitious, they will be kissing-up.

They need to see you and your role separately if they ever hope to be better than you are in your role. But—

- They must never neglect their obligation to get better and better in their own roles.
- They might wish to prepare themselves for more responsibility. But they need to do this primarily by demonstrating responsibility for performing their own roles superlatively.
- The better you are in your role, the higher you set the bar for them. This is the way it should be. If you are incompetent, and they are ambitious, they will end up being less competent than you were.

Where to Go from Here

In a typical ("pyramidal") organization, those members of the CEO's staff have staffs of their own. Once these four covenants are set and functioning in this top piece of the organization, it is now time to go to the next level.

Each of the CEO's staff establishes the four covenants with his or her subordinates in their piece of the organization. They should do so in much the same way as described above. Their advantage is that they have weathered the process as subordinates, so they can probably improve upon the process.

This process should cascade down in every piece of the organization. This needs to continue until every person at every level is performing in accord with these four covenants.

New hires need to be apprised of this way of doing things before they sign on. Every promotion needs to be based on these four covenants, whether it is within or from without the organization.

The primary advantage of using the four covenants as a "tool" for developing a fully competent organization is that it makes clear what needs to be aligned with in general.

You would be better off in your pursuit of the organization's mission to use these as a basis for mentoring people than using non-repeatable achievements or shortfalls. The achievements and the shortfalls are then those that are specific to the role descriptions, and to the four covenants.

The best performance measurements are always those that relate to prior agreements—in this case, the role descriptions and the four covenants.

How to Test the Integrity of the Four Covenants

You will want to know how the covenants are working—that is, how deeply they have been taken in, and what evidence there is of how they are being implemented.

- Assume you have entered into these four covenants with "Mother"—the spirit of your organization past, present, and future . . . *which you MUST do.*
- Then *you* must be the ideal example of how to live daily by these four covenants.
- It is not so much that your people will try to emulate you—although there will always be a few who do try. It is that when you are directly experiencing the challenges of living up to the covenants *you* have entered-into, you will be on far better ground to mentor your people.
- What you don't learn, you can't teach.

- You will be able to discern how capable your people are of living up to the covenants they have made by the quality of the questions they ask—of themselves, of you and others, and of the best there have ever been in the role they are in.
- How well you keep your covenants will go far toward determining how well your people will keep theirs. And how well they keep theirs will essentially determine how well they are going to make covenants with their own people.

Why covenants?

Competent people use covenants with themselves as their guidance system. Organizations are collectives. So it is the covenants made within those organizations that provide their guidance systems.

A high level of performance in any endeavor is almost always associated with being committed to something greater than oneself. Covenants provide this kind of impetus. The aim is the performance of the organization. You can't make a fully competent organization without a tool such as these four covenants.

Some Basics to Ponder Further

- If your people are not capable of fulfilling their roles in the pursuit of the organization's purpose for being, that could well be because you are not capable of fulfilling yours. Commitment begins with you.
- If you don't hire and cast people who can make such commitments as the four covenants, you probably can't have a fully competent organization.
- If, when all else fails, you can't or won't, or they can't or don't, it's time to make some painful changes.
- There is only one measure of commitment. And that is *performance.*
- Merely "having" a purpose is wishful thinking. Being *had by* your purpose makes it a *necessity.* The organizational equivalent has to do with such covenants as these.
- *Hopes and desires are not a method.*

14. *Thinking* Tools and Techniques

Let us take an intermission from orchestrating the kinds of tools and techniques required for making competent organizations—in order to be reminded of first things.

The tools and techniques we focus on here that might be put to use are all indispensable. What we can use this intermission for is to remind ourselves and review such concepts as:

No tool or technique can be any better than its users.

What this means is that the master tool is always the mind of the leader, and that the master techniques always derive from the way that particular leader thinks. How the leader thinks determines who he or she IS. And who the leader IS will determine what he or she does.

That's why tidy recipes—in the form of "the secrets of . . ." or "the six principles for success" don't work. Leaders are often quite different from one another. It is only "mediocre" people who are similar. They copy one another. Leaders know that even the "best practices" may not work with them or in their unique organizations.

To have a competent organization requires it to be orchestrated in such a way that it invariably exceeds the expectations of its users and stakeholders. How this is done in any organization depends upon many factors that are never a part of a standardized "recipe." The main factors will always be how the leader thinks, and how a particular organization's culture makes certain things possible, other things necessary, and still others irrelevant.

It is the way the CEO thinks that ultimately determines what kind of muscle and resiliency the organization will have. Before moving on with our exploration of the unique tools and techniques required for making uniquely competent organizations, let us pause and reconsider the key tool—how the leader thinks about what needs thinking about:

- *Before all else, the best leaders are strategic communicators.* What this means is that you never enter into any communication situation—from casual conversations to reading to speaking before others—without carefully strategizing the process in advance. This begins with having a clear conception of what you are trying to accomplish. The "strategy" lies in devising the means for getting from the outset to that accomplishment.

  It is not enough to have a strategy for accomplishment. You must also have the skills to carry it out. This calls for a seemingly infinite capacity for improvising. Like battlefield "strategies," no strategy will outlast the initial engagement. Things are always changing. When you read, for example, *you* are changing moment by moment as a result of how you are interpreting what you are reading.

  You have plotted your course. You will always be deflected from it. The challenge to your competence as a communicator will always be how to get back on course from wherever you are deflected.

  This requires mental agility and communicative resources. Those who don't have them get thrown off their path and can't get back on it.

Strategic communication is based on the *need to know.* You are either providing other people with what they need to know, or providing yourself with what you need to know. They have an agenda, you have an agenda, and the organization—on-behalf-of which you are communicating—has an agenda. Communication strategies have to do with aligning these so they are pulling together in the same direction.

Communication strategies are always a function of the relationships involved. So the strategies precede by far the encounter itself. The right relationships will facilitate the right outcomes. So maintain those prior to any encounter.

For example, if you are a poor reader or listener, you are already in a relationship with authors or others that will impede your effectiveness.

Underlying all of this, it is how leaders talk to themselves that sets the discipline and the possibilities. If you are not leading yourself in your inner, private conversations, there is very little likelihood that you will be able to lead others—no matter your strategy. If you can't convince yourself, you probably can't convince others.

- Closely related is the leadership task of *managing meaning*. All communication is based on interpretations, whether you are on the "sending" side or the "receiving" side. There may be facts, but those always have to be interpreted. Facts are meaningless apart from how they are interpreted. It is the interpretation that provides the meanings that people live by, think by, and work by.

  The leader's task—and opportunity—is to manipulate their own and others' interpretations in such a way that they move the organization forward in the direction it needs to go.

  The question is never "What is going on?" It is "How should we be interpreting whatever is going on to our short- and long-term interests advantage?" The question is never "What does this *mean?*" It is "What kind of meaning do we need to assign to this that furthers our mission?"

  This is not just the leader's prerogative. It is the leader's obligation. Some meaning will be assigned to everything and everyone. It is the leader's task to "manage" the meanings first he or she and then others assign to things. The "organization" cannot do this. Leaders have to do this on-behalf-of their organizations. That's the primary duty of being the chief steward of the organization's present and thus its future.

  The *right* meaning—the one that drives the organization forward toward its cause—has to be assigned to everything. The more competent your people, the more potent the organization's culture will be. If people are putting just the right meaning to things, you need to say nothing. If they don't, you need to intervene.

You don't want your voice to be the loudest one. It just needs to be the one that makes certain the right meaning gets put on things. For example, calling something a problem may lead you into a diversion. You may want to take the position that "This came our way. How can we use it to our advantage?"

At sea, the winds and the current may not be favorable. On land, this may be "the economy." It makes no difference. You still have to make way on your course. All kinds of excuses lurk in arbitrary interpretations. Don't let that happen.

Meanings are supported by the stories that are made up to support them. Make certain that the stories you tell, and that others' tell, support the needs and interests of the organization and not some other purpose. Plausible stories are created to support how people think—or would like to think. Or, how people believe. Change the story, change the meaning of things.

- Also closely related is the idea of Return on Attention (ROA) At the end of the day, you will be a sum total of what you have paid attention to all day long. In much the same way, the organization will become a cumulative result of what its people pay attention to all day. *Control your attention, control your life.*

When they don't—or can't—do this for themselves, it becomes a leaders' task to do it for them. Fully competent people are good at determining what needs paying attention to. Less competent people typically aren't.

You are the chief navigator. If people are not paying attention to what they should be paying attention to, make it possible—and *necessary*—for them to do so. You can do this by good example, and by intolerance. You have to be intolerant of people who consistently pay attention to the wrong things.

THE COMPETENT ORGANIZATION

Every conversation you have with people is an opportunity for coaching or mentoring them. Make this central to all of your coaching and mentoring.

- People don't just "have" habits. Our habits "have' us, in the sense that they take us where *they* go. Habits are more powerful than desire or intentions. Habits determine our perceptions, our conceptions, and our actions.

You can't "motivate" people to think or do something that their habits preclude. Nor can you "motivate" yourself to think or do something that your habits preclude.

Thus what always needs fixing is people's habits. You cannot directly influence habits. You can only change them by displacing them with other habits. When you do this for yourself, you will have all the insight you need into how to go about changing others' habits.

The only other way you have of doing this is to make an alternative habit possible—but also *necessary*. When competent people see a habit of theirs that needs breaking, they "break" it by replacing it with a better habit for their purposes.

When you see a habit that is working against the movement of the organization in its rightful direction, you need to do the same. Make it impossible to follow a wrong habit. And then make it possible to follow a better one. And then make it *necessary* in some way to do so.

In an organization, a habit is a routine regularly in charge—whether that is a way of thinking, a way of seeing, or a way of doing. Make the routine impossible, and you can break the "habit."

What is not a habit is not sustainable. Thus you need the habits that make the competence of the organization sustainable. You just have to have the right habits, which will extinguish the wrong ones. Don't look to pop psych recipes for this. Go for what actually drives behavior—habits.

LEE THAYER

- Closely related here are "mental models." Our experiences create our minds. And minds create mental models—that is, routine ways of thinking about things, understanding things, or doing something about them. They are like theories. We see the world in terms of the theories we have for seeing that world.

A mental model not only imposes its own meanings on the world. It tells us what to do about it.

When mental models become crystallized, they are not subject to change even though the evidence for their inadequacy is blatantly obvious. As the old adage goes, people become set in their ways. When they do, their mental models go from being slightly wrong to being dead wrong.

This will happen to you if you ever fall out of the "learning mode." Treat your own mental models as no more than hypotheses about the world. They are thus always subject to change as circumstances change. Approach every situation as if you have never encountered it before. Learn how to deal with it. Then forget it, to deal with the next situation afresh.

Great leaders are *learners*, not *knowers*. They never take their own mental models for granted. They put those mental models to the test every time, to determine in what way they are inadequate or obsolete, given the circumstances.

They also teach their people how to do the same thing. Never assume that your mental models are adequate or accurate. As Alexander the Great taught us, every situation is different. Learn to deal with the situation. Don't impose a prior mental model on it.

Competent organizations—infused as they are with competent people—avoid "success paradigms," as they have been called.

Success in a prior situation does not guarantee success in a present situation.

Mental models are useful. They make dealing with the real world more efficient. But leaders never sacrifice effectiveness for efficiency.

THE COMPETENT ORGANIZATION

And the best leaders avoid stereotypes—whether about people or situations.

- There has been much in the preceding pages about **becoming**. This is the operant term in competent organizations. People are continuously *becoming* better. The organization is continuously *becoming* better.

  Role descriptions are about becoming—about what the person or the organization will *become* over time. We wrongly evaluate people by who they *are* and how they are performing in the present. It is their growth that we need to measure. It is the pace of the growth in their competence that we need to measure.

  Everyone—like every thing—is always in the process of becoming. It is what they will become that makes a difference in the long-term performance of the organization—not what they are at the moment.

  Today is obviously critical. But leaders are always focused on tomorrow. It is what the organization will be capable of tomorrow that determines the organization's destiny. That forward thinking distinguishes the most competent leaders. Mediocre leaders are always mired in the events of the day. They may say they are too busy putting out today's fires to be able to think much about tomorrow. But what today's fires become tomorrow is the issue.

  People may believe they "deserve" better. But the best perspective on this is as follows:

  "If you want to know what kind of organization (or life) you 'deserve,' look at the one you've got."

  In other words, you will 'deserve' what comes your way tomorrow because you did not create tomorrow. You merely let it happen to you.

  Great leaders are not event-driven. They are purpose-driven. And a purpose can only be realized by focusing on it—by focusing on tomorrow even more than today. Today is pretty much history because it was determined by yesterday.

You can create tomorrow only by being obsessed about it.
Tomorrow is always the next step in the journey. People who are
not engaged in their future cannot engage fully in their present.
They live a life of distraction.

- The theme of **necessity** also runs through much of the preceding pages of this book.

There is good reason for this. People are full of hopes and dreams for themselves and for the real world they have to engage. But great leaders think about it this way: things happen for one of two reasons:

1. They are more or less random or fortuitous; or
2. They are necessary.

Great leaders have always described their cause as _necessary_. They have seen themselves as the _necessary_ instrument of their necessary purposes. They know that happenstance (or "luck") is always a player in the real world. The world does not pitch in just because they are passionate about their cause or purposes. In fact, you only encounter great obstacles if you have a great and worthy purpose. If you are just floating through life, you will encounter very little resistance.

The Wright brothers experienced many failures. They had to figure out how to overcome the resistance of air to their attempts to penetrate it. The sheer resistance they encountered did not give way because they were so determined. It didn't give way at all. They had to design a way to overcome it.

The real world is that way. It is the way it is because it is necessarily so. Even a couch potato will remain at rest until it is _necessary_ for him or her to move. Their destination may be the bathroom or a snack. Whatever. The forces that kept them at rest had to be overcome by some greater necessity.

Leaders who are _had by_ their cause—rather than merely _having_ some purpose—carries with it a force of nature equivalent to what the leader will encounter along the way. That makes the leader irrepressible. If the leader is imaginative and clever, this permits him or her to overcome most of the obstacles encountered.

It is the power of being inexorably driven. Merely "having" a purpose is puny by comparison.

- And the concept of **learning** is fundamental.

Learning is either a habit, or it will atrophy. Students perennially struggle with learning for "the exam." When learning is not a habit, it takes great effort to make it work in the short term. In the long term, it will not be cumulative.

A central product of learning is that it enables you to learn more. It is not the content that matters. It is the process.

That is why we have emphasized here what we're calling "the learning mode." That is a set of habits that drives irrepressible curiosity about anything that might bear upon one's cause in life.

If a person has no cause in life, then it doesn't matter what you learn. So we go to school and to activities that used to be called "adult education."

Education is when someone else tells you what you should know.

Learning is relevant only when you have a cause in life and have to (out of necessity!) learn how to achieve it. Think of examples like Abraham Lincoln, or Thomas Edison. Or Cleopatra. She had to learn how to accomplish what she did. No one could have taught her that.

Great leaders have always had to *learn* what they needed to know to accomplish what they did.

It is the same for competent people and for competent organizations. There is no way of "teaching" people how to be great. Unique individuals in unique circumstances have to "teach" themselves. This is called learning.

Those who would accomplish what has not been accomplished before have to learn in one of two ways:

1. By learning from the mistakes of others who have gone before them; and/or
2. By learning from their own mistakes.

We try to learn from our predecessors' successes. This doesn't work. We are not them. And we do not live in the circumstances they lived in. But we could learn from their mistakes.

Most people can't do this. Most people don't even ask. Incompetent people ask for a no-effort recipe provided by a guru or a celebrity.

What's most important to remember here is that most adults are neither interested in nor capable of any real learning—the kind of learning that reorganizes their minds and enables them to think differently. They will be your employees. If it is not *necessary* for them to learn how to learn, they won't.

To learn, you have to learn how to fail and profit from it. Most people are simply learning-aversive for this reason. Education is tested by paper-and-pencil tests.

It is learning that is tested in the real world that competent people and competent organizations require.

- People who are committed to some kind of purpose for their lives will understand that an organization can have a purpose for its existence. People who do not themselves live purposefully cannot understand this.

What leaders have had to learn the hard way over the centuries is that this leaves them with two possibilities:

1. Either bring their purposes into alignment with those of the organization. This can be done only by casting them in a role that simultaneously serves both purposes; or
2. If they have none, make it *necessary* for them to adopt the purposes of the organization.

There is no feasible third option if you intend to have a competent organization. People will thrive only if they are serving some master greater than themselves. This could be their own good and worthy purposes. Or it could be the destiny of your organization.

Leaders know it has to be one or the other.

People must be stewards of some cause greater than themselves if they are to have relevant and worthy lives.

- There has been too much talk about **incentives**, and even more misleading talk about **motivation**.

It is well to remember that those terms came from lab work with rats at Harvard University years ago. For the most part, people are not rats. People write academic papers about rats. But rats do not write academic papers about people.

It is when the intent is to manipulate people's performance that the sham becomes transparent. There was a review of all such things some years ago entitled *Punished by Rewards*. The conclusion was that rewards, incentives, and the like actually backfired most of the time. It was wishful thinking to believe that they would not.

Not only did they not work as hoped (wishful thinking), but in most cases caused a *decline* in performance and morale.

What you need to know is that competent people do not have to be either prodded or enticed to perform. They try to outperform themselves without any outside sticks or carrots.

Incompetent people, on the other hand, may work a little harder for a reward of some sort. But they will not work smarter. And they will end up being dependent on the reward, and resent being treated like rats.

As for "motivation": leaders don't place any faith in "motivation"—whatever that is. They know that *necessity* is a far stronger force.

What separates piano virtuosos from run-of-the-mill piano players is not "motivation." It is longer hours and years of practice. You cannot "motivate" people to be great performers. That requires competence, mastery, and beyond.

External incentives may nudge marginally-competent people into being adequate performers. But it is people who sustain (or not) the commitment to get better. If it is necessary—*for them*—they will do what needs to be done.

You can't "pull" people into superior performance. They have to "push" themselves.

- Competent people are curious. Incompetent people assume they know it all. So competent people are ingenious **question-askers**. Incompetent people assume they have no need to ask questions.

  Successful leaders, for example, ask about four questions to every statement they make. Marginally-adequate leaders make about four statements to every question they ask. Even then, their questions are not provocative. They do not move things forward.

- Closely intertwined with the learning mode is the willingness to let the situation and its logic define themselves. Learners do not impose their mental models on the world. They ask questions to allow the real world to impose **its logic** on them.

  Incompetent people are arrogant. They want to impose whatever they happen to know on the world. If it doesn't fit, they expect someone to fix the world so their well-worn mental models will work. They are highly prejudiced about anything that does not fit their own beliefs. They are quick to stereotype people and situations. The prefer to decide first and then complain about the facts.

Competent people—and thus competent organizations—are quite the opposite.

Competent people—and thus competent organizations—learn from the **logic** of the real world. They play by the logic of reality, not the logic of their beliefs "about it."

That is a prerequisite of competent organizations.

- Competent organizations are throughout **accomplishment-minded**. They navigate not by their feelings or their predispositions, but by what they are trying to accomplish.

  Their activities are in the service of the accomplishments they are pursuing. Others less competent make the activities most important and the untoward results not their fault.

  Competent people—whether they are reading, listening, or talking—produce the circumstances needed for what they intend to accomplish.

  The accomplishment intended is the navigational star. Most internal problems arise from not being on some consistent and persistent course.

  Incompetent people—and thus incompetent organizations—do not want to be constrained by the *purpose* of a conversation or an encounter. They want to be "free" to do "their own thing." More organizations fail than succeed. That is most often the reason.

  So what were you trying to accomplish in these five paragraphs?

- **"Competence."** That is what this book is all about—competent people and competent organizations.

What is it? It is the ability and the resources to perceive the world on its own terms, and to invent a way to achieve the objective *in spite of* whatever unexpected obstacles arise.

How is it to be measured? It has to be measured in terms of outcomes. Competence does not always win. But it generates a track record far superior to the indifference of incompetence.

Competent people—and thus competent organizations—learn from their failures. They know that the "fix" is *in here* and not *out there*.

If competence is so desirable, why is it so rare? It is rare because cultures always establish the "norms." If competence were normative, there would plenty of it. As it is, the larger culture actually encourages incompetence. For example, we are into remedies, not prevention. In schools, it is the incompetent pupils who get the most attention. In their advertising, pharmaceuticals tell us how to ameliorate symptoms (which are always on the increase). We are a "sick" society because we come at it from that direction—everyone needs to treat every ailment.

The leanings of a culture always reflect the weight of numbers. If you have a culture of incompetence in your organization, you will get more of that. If you can manage to develop a culture of competence in your organization, you will get more of that.

Our culture says we are "victims" of this or that, beyond our control.

Competent people—like competent organizations—play the opposite game: what shall we do to avoid being "victims" of happenings presumed to be beyond our control?

And about ROA:

In her book *Distracted: The Erosion of Attention* . . . , Maggie Jackson wrote:

> *"As we cultivate lives of distraction, we are losing our capacity to create and preserve wisdom . . . and slipping towards a line of ignorance that is paradoxically born of an abundance of information and connectivity."*

15. More Tools and Techniques: III

Those to be considered in this chapter are about **communication** and about **values and beliefs.**

For people to relate or to collaborate, some form of communication is required. It is in communication that our own minds are formed and infected by others. And it is in communication that we infect the minds of others. We are who we are because others communicate with us as they do. And we are enabled and constrained by how we communicate with ourselves—our ever-private conversations with ourselves.

We think like we do in large part because the others with whom we are routinely in communication think like they do. If we agree with them, we like them. If we don't agree with them, they do not become our friends.

We partake of what's being talked about around us, and from the outpourings of the various media. We choose what to imbibe, and what to ignore.

We are thus organized the way our communication networks organize us. We can advantageously think of communication as the organizing principle and mechanisms underlying all organizations—from a simple relationship to a complex multi-thousand person corporation or government agency.

The key is always: Who can say what to whom, with what results? That is what structures our worlds—whether intentionally (as in formal organizations) or inadvertently (as in the chance encounters we have with others, of whatever length). We are led by how others communicate with us, and how we communicate with others and with ourselves. That maps the world for us, and provides us with good or poor tools for navigating those worlds.

Leadership lies primarily in the meaning of things. So it is necessary for leaders to be the master managers of meaning—for themselves and for others.

What we don't "know" can hurt us. What we do "know" can also hurt us. This is as pertinent to organizations as it is to individuals.

What we *don't* know can hurt us if we have a need to know for our own individual or collective purposes. What we *do* know can hurt us if it is misleading, or simply wrong (given our individual or collective purposes).

Those who assume that communication is a trivial but intuitive process are either dead or wrong, or both.

It is the process by which we get to where we want to go (or don't get to where we want to go). It is the vital, the conscious life, process.

It is never incidental to the life of a person or an organization. It is *always* inescapably consequential to the life of an individual or an organization.

This is why great leaders have also been great communicators. And why their organizations have been astoundingly superior. They gave communication—which gives us the only conscious reality we can have—its due.

Surveillance

Let's start from the outside in. Every sentient critter—including we humans—has to maintain a communicative grasp of the environment. That's where both the dangers and the opportunities lie. We have to avoid predators if we can. And, for reasons of economics or status or power or food, or for reasons of ideology or politics, we all sometimes function as predators.

We do this as individuals. And we do this in any kind of human grouping. In the modern world, we face the ongoing dilemma of influencing others or being influenced by them. Having money translates into having status and power. We are heavily influenced by our personal celebrities and by the impersonal commercial media. We may not know our neighbors in the same building or on the same block. But we get our news about what is going on in the world primarily from the "experts" and from gossip.

If CEOs get together, they talk shop. It's a form of gossip. They influence one another. That's why they and their organizations are so similar. It is mutual predation, to determine who "wins" the game of being superior. The richest ones usually win. But sometimes it is the most convincing (a communication characteristic).

We may not actually "lie." But communication is always gamey. We deceive when it appears to us to be in our best interest to do so. We strut and preen. Leadership, even of a conversation, is always a performing art. We play our roles to be convincing. We play our roles to advantage ourselves, no matter how small a pond we swim in.

We need to know how others think, and what their strategies seem to be, so we can figure out a strategy of "one-upmanship."

Still, in the midst of all this chicanery, we need to know that the world we see "out there" is pretty much the same as others see. They may be wrong. We may all be wrong. But we will share a worldview. It is the basis for all of our petty—and even crucial—conversations.

We have this from the ironies of the writer Cyril Connolly (1903-1974):

> *"All charming people have something to conceal, usually their total dependence on the appreciation of others."*

CEOs heed this: The higher your status, the more dependent you are on the appreciation (real or otherwise) of others. Your status can be either enabling or disabling. It depends upon how you use it.

We can all be caught up short in the observations of the journalist/ muckraker H L Mencken ((1880-1956) who wrote:

*"It is hard to believe that a man is telling the truth when you know
that you would lie if you were in his place."*

What this might suggest is that a person who has lied might therefore be
unduly skeptical of others. On the other hand, if you had never lied, you
would be an easy mark for others' lies. The cleverest person is the one who
best conceals it.

We know that all of this goes on apace in every organization every day.
Modern organizations are heavily politicized. Research shows that
chimpanzees (some say our closest relative) are political creatures. But they
have not as many ways to deceive as humans have. We do not live in a
natural world, but in the world of words.

All of this is in the way of saying that surveillance (or reconnaissance—
preliminary survey or research) by organizations is fraught with difficulties
for two reasons:

1. One is the complex compartmentalization of modern organizations.
    People work in their own group "silos." They are territorial and
    political. Their internal machinations get in the way of looking
    outward. No one, it seems, is looking out for the interest of the
    organization as a whole. Even the CEO is insulated from the world
    by his or her aides, who often have in mind their own agendas, not
    the organization's agenda.

2. In our "modern" world, people are not brought up to put the
    health and welfare of the family ahead of their own, or that of
    their relationships, or of their classrooms, or of the organizations
    on which they depend for their own livelihood—even though it
    is in their own best self-interests to do so. We have been educated
    into smaller and smaller niches. We see the world from the biases of
    our own meager experiences and our own limited preoccupations.

So we literally do not know what to look for out there in the environment,
or how to interpret it.

Chimpanzee groups are more vulnerable than are ant colonies. Is that because chimpanzee groups are more busily engaged in internal politics and struggles for status to be aware of threats to the whole? Our own society seems to be rotting from the inside. How does *that* get on the national agenda?

Such problems and obstacles face the CEO of any organization. Adequate surveillance is critical to the health and welfare of the organization. So, how to do it? Here is one way that works:

- Create an "organizational intelligence" group. This would consist of all of the key functional managers. They in turn would recruit all of their people to provide inputs and observations.
- They would independently provide surveillance from their perspectives. Be certain that all the domains are covered—economic/financial, operational, competitor, customer/marketing, stakeholder, social, technological, regulatory, political, global and local. What you want here is anything that appears it might bear upon the mission of the organization in any or all of its parts.
- Make sure the scanner is competent—that is, that they know what they are looking for and how to interpret it. As we have all learned, this is more challenging than it appears. Train and develop those scanners and one or more backups.
- Require that they provide a daily intelligence report covering all of the specialized media. This may consist of zero concerns to a long list of concerns. You don't want *all* of your managers reading the *Wall Street Journal.* After making sure all of the relevant sources have been covered, it is enough to have one scanner who reports to all others who have a *need to know.*
- Via internal logistics, this intelligence must be brought to the attention of any and all of those who have a *need to know.* The logistics of all internal intelligence should be based on *need to know.*
- Those who receive need-to-know intelligence should then report to their "boss" what the concern is and what they are doing about it. This needs to funnel and be distilled until it reaches the CEO. All you want to know is this: what is going on that might bear upon our cause and its path, and what is being done about it—by whom?

- The problem and its solutions needs to be **owned** by someone and not the CEO. His or her task is to know what is being done in order to calculate the appropriate overall strategies.

What's important here is that any threat or opportunity needs to be anticipated with the longest advance alert possible, and that someone is responsible for suggesting what should be done about it.

This is often assumed in conventional organizations. And sometimes, when not much changes in the environment that bears upon the organization's cause and mission, it works adequately. But a carefully conceptualized framework such as this can insure that nothing ends up being a surprise.

Anticipating the unexpected is the result you want. How you get there can be improvised from the above. The important thing is that you have a system and a scheme for surveillance, ownership of the problem, and adequate reaction time.

What threatens the life and destiny of the organization is almost always unexpected. The opportunities that pop up are even more elusive. It is the quality and the comprehensiveness of your surveillance system that alerts those who have a need to know. It isn't the bare information that the CEO needs to know. It is how sound the interpretation is and what is being done about it that the CEO needs to know.

With an adequate intelligence system in place and empowered by competence, the CEO has no need to read the *Wall Street Journal* or the local newspaper. This is being done for him or her. Leaders need to have their heads above water all the time. They cannot afford to have their attention diverted from the overall health and welfare of the organization today—and tomorrow. A good and competent organizational intelligence system takes them off a furtive watch into comprehensive oversight.

Relating to Customers and Other Stakeholders

Then, let's look from the inside out.

There are five major targets that should be of concern to any CEO (or the head of any organization).

- Your customers or clients. Of equal importance, your *prospective* customers or clients. You want them to know what problem(s) of theirs you can solve better than anyone else. You communicate this to them best by the growing reputation of your organization, and the reputations of your products and/or services. Take care of that first.

- Whether you have 5 or 50,000 employees, enlist them all in your marketing/sales efforts. If they are proud of their part in making available your products and/or services, they can be your most effective and efficient salespeople. This requires two things: that they know as much about your products and/or services as you do. And second, that they get some coaching in how to tell their families and friends. Should they get "paid" for their accomplishments outside of their regular role descriptions? Absolutely! But never in money. Always in some other form. [This might be, for example, one of the criteria for their personal Appreciated Value Index—described a bit later. Or they might receive tuition assistance, or an account for their learning plans.]

- Your suppliers should always be aware of who you are, where you are headed, and how you are going to get there. They, too, would like to have more competent organizations. And since the two of you are tied together in your transactions, you could help them to get better at these and thus at everything they do. This is a win-win.

- Your competitors (as is true of your "enemies," as every military strategist has known for centuries) has a more accurate view of you than do your friends, your board members, or your suppliers. They all have a vested interest in your success. This makes your competitors' views invaluable to you. Acquire those perspectives whenever and however you can, even directly. If you want to *change* their perceptions, never try to do so directly. Do so via the media that you have in common. Make sure that they read the stories about you (or receive the rumors about you) are the ones you want *them* to have. This is along the lines of the old adage: "Keep your friends close, but your enemies closer."

- We live in an age when the public—or even your own employees— won't believe you unless they see it in the newspapers or on TV. The battlefield for winning minds and hearts is there. Learn how to tell your story. Learn how to place it in the right channels of distribution. Some would call this "public relations." It is much more than that. These are the battles you must win if you wish to win the war. These are the arenas of mind-making and heart-taking you must master if you want to "get your message across." Forget the slogans on the walls of your offices and workplaces. People tend to believe only what they see or read in the media. This is where all the strategies play out these days.

Internal Logistics

We alluded to this above. How do you move just the right information—or better, "intelligence" around inside your organization?

Almost all communication is a form of propaganda. People always have an agenda in mind. They are always trying to achieve something with other people—whether they are aware of it or not. They are the source of propaganda (could be "gossip"), and they are the targets of others' propaganda.

Your primary task here is to participate unbeknownst to others in these everyday loops—if for no other reason than to be aware of what constitutes reality for the various groups of people in your organization. You won't find their reality in your head. It is only in their heads.

If you need to change the meanings of things (which we have explored previously), you have to do so in the communication systems and channels that your people use every day.

You have to have the "intelligence" you need to know what the facts are for your people. You can't change what the facts mean to them directly. You have to do so here, where they have their source and where they are maintained—in the communication systems which they regularly participate in.

It might be nice if they spoke more candidly with you about their opinions of things. It might be nice if you could speak more candidly with them about *your* concerns and interests. But you and they live in two different worlds. They go online to talk about you and your organization—right or wrong. They rarely go online to talk *to* you. And they don't inhabit the world you do.

No one does this better than Machiavelli (have you read his work recently?), or Gracian, as in his 17th-century book, *The Art of Worldly Wisdom.* If you want something more current, try F. G. Bailey, *Humbuggery and Manipulation: The Art of Leadership,* or any of Elbert Hubbard's musings.

The reason rationality doesn't work in the real world is that few people are capable of being rational, and then only in short spurts as scientists sometimes do.

Still, how you handle the logistics of information and intelligence internally and with your stakeholders will underwrite the possibilities for your being able to make a competent organization. Plant the meanings you want people to cling to in the stories you tell. Telling people the "facts" either puts them to sleep or raises their hackles.

The best approach to communication may be by the methods of epidemiology. The great leader and thinker Seneca (4 B.C.-65 A.D.) put it cleverly when he wrote:

> *"Nobody will keep the thing he hears to himself, and nobody will repeat just what he hears and no more."*

People are always editorializing (adding their opinions). Make sure they do so in your favor. The more your relationships are *like* love affairs, the more influence you will have. In other words, people will "love" you if they are convinced you "love" them. But be sure you love for what they *ought to become*, and not what they *are* today (as the German poet and philosopher Goethe suggested).

It's an unsurpassable tool where communication is concerned.

Values and beliefs are also among the key tools for making competent organizations.

All people live—more or less—according to their values and beliefs. Most of these are derived from the larger culture to which they belong, from their communication networks and media sources, and from their associates at work.

Most values and beliefs become shared with little or no prodding. If you grew up in an exclusively French-speaking home, you would be a French speaker. By the time you became a teenager, your friends influence your values and beliefs more than your parents do. "When in Rome, most will do as the Romans do." We pick up our values and beliefs primarily from those around us, and from the media we mutually imbibe.

If you were a Navy Seal, your values and beliefs would either have gotten you in, or may on revelation get you kicked out. You were selected because you had the right kind of values and beliefs. These got fine-tuned implicitly. It is as if they were in the water and the air. Actually, they were implicit in the way people communicated with you, and the way they expected you to communicate with yourself and with others.

People in small communities often share the same values and beliefs. If they don't, they can't really "belong."

But in a world in which most of the sources of our values and beliefs are anonymous, the rationale for "belonging" has to be more explicit. We live in an infinitely-disintegrating society. The people who come into your organization have sometimes widely-divergent backgrounds.

If they are to "belong" to your organization, you may have to make explicit the values and beliefs they espouse and enact.

You can practice as much "diversity" as you want. But if your people do not share the values and beliefs that are crucial to the organization's future, its future will forever be uncertain.

For these compelling reasons, you should consider a written document setting forth the values and beliefs your organization needs to fulfill its cause. Your posture in this is not at all "These are the values and beliefs we practice." Rather, it should be, "These are the values and beliefs every member of this organization should aspire to every day."

Pull people in that direction. Do not push them. And do not assume that, just because they say so, people have internalized them. The only evidence that you can rely on is that people *enact* these particular values and beliefs in their everyday comportment.

To cite the German poet and philosopher Goethe (18th-19th century) once again,

> *"Everything that emancipates the spirit without giving control over ourselves is harmful."*

This might be taken to mean that values and beliefs that do not give us more control over ourselves may lead us in the wrong direction. Or, that the freedom to think and speak for ourselves may reduce our control over ourselves.

It is paradoxical. The greater the cause to which we might devote our lives, the more self-discipline is required.

So there would necessarily be much in any good statement of values and beliefs that would point people in the direction of self-control and self-discipline. What's of value is learning and growth. Beliefs that deny this may be harmful, as Goethe says.

For sure, people are not in business to produce "philosophies." But if they are not guided by the right kinds of philosophies, they suffer. The right set of values and beliefs is one that grows and enriches our humanity at the same time as it grows and enriches a healthy, purposeful organization, and one that is rewarded in the same measure.

A random example of a line item from a statement of values and beliefs may be useful:

- *We believe that good work, superbly done, is the richest source of human dignity and of quality of life.*

Here's how we might "unpack" this, which needs to be a part of every statement of values and beliefs:

> *The lesson of history is that being fully engaged with one's work is the path to being engaged fully as a human being with life. Every other path has been tried. None has produced the sense of being fully alive, of full human dignity, that comes from good work, competently carried out, superbly done. This does not mean working "harder." In fact, it means the opposite. The more competent you are, the easier, the more fun, and the more rewarding will be your work. You spend the bulk of your waking hours at work. Those hours dominate the rest of your life. The life you cannot have at work is a life you cannot have.*

*One thing is certain: Mediocre work will **always** result in a mediocre life.*

Meaningful work. There is nothing that can contribute more to a meaningful life. It is not the social importance of your work. It is solely in how competently you perform at work.

Whether you are the yardman or the CEO: good work is everywhere the attitude you bring to it. And that is always a consequence of the renewed and enhanced competence you bring to your work every day.

Yes, that sounds "idealistic." But that's what values and beliefs are: ideals. Not ideals just to think about and talk about. But ideals to be achieved in the way people perform their roles.

If you don't aim for the ideal, you will always end up in some lesser place in life.

[The balance of this particular example of values and beliefs is offered in Appendix B as "Our Guiding Values and Beliefs." This is certainly not the only way to do it. But it can be taken as an *example* of *how* it might be done.]

As stated earlier, such a statement is not a bragging statement about how superior your organization is. It is a statement that establishes the values and beliefs you intend for those in your organization to constantly aspire to. It "pulls," it does not "push."

The leader must embody the values and beliefs he or she intends others to rise up to. Or at least be seen as striving to do so, making observable daily progress.

Every leader in the organization must be seen to live by these values and beliefs, or at least striving daily to do so.

That is what makes it possible to expect that all others will use these values and beliefs as navigational stars, by which attitudes and character will be measured.

They must become a part of indoctrination sessions for newcomers. They must become a part of how people who have been members longer are evaluated. With each passing year, more evidence of how they are navigating their work and their lives by these values and beliefs should be expected. After a year, they should be expected to *mentor* others who are junior to them about these values and beliefs.

Competence is to be measured not just by how productive people are, but by *how* they perform their roles.

It is a way of belonging—to each other and to the organization—which cannot be gotten in any other way.

"Trust"

It has become very popular in recent years to refer to "trust" as a method. *Never, ever, use trust as a method or a technique to "incentivize" team or individual performance.*

In competent organizations, trust has to be earned. You can trust people who are fully competent. You cannot "trust" people who are not. You can trust people who perform. You cannot trust people who don't.

Less than competent people often use loyalty or "trust" to hide their shortfalls. You cannot discern from talk. Many people who are not competent in their roles are good talkers.

If you think about it as follows, you cannot go wrong:

> *The only reliable measure of competence is performance.*
> *Or, alternatively, the only real measure of performance is performance.*

At the same time, you must always keep your faith in people up to the moment you cut them lose for continuing failure to perform as agreed. Be positive until you have to be terminally negative. All your talk about under-performance doesn't accomplish much. Other people's performance is not your problem. It is theirs. Make it necessary for them to own their performance *and* their assessment of it.

Make certain they know they own it. Then you can support and, on rare occasions, bring them around. Let them *own* their performance failures. Then it will work like a kick in the pants. But you should never take on the role of the bad cop. That may be the way things are done in conventional organizations.

But it has no place if you intend to make a competent organization.

Should you trust yourself? You are entitled to do so only if you have demonstrated your trustworthiness over a long period of time.

If you yourself are not trustworthy, you cannot make it necessary for others to be trustworthy.

This will appear again in **Appendix B** in the example given there of "Our Guiding Values and Beliefs."

Trust is valuable. But only if the people involved can trust each other to perform their roles competently. After all else is considered, it is probably the reason why the Special Forces are typically so effective.

16. More Tools and Techniques: IV

The organization IS the way it works.
Change the way it works, and you change the organization.

Change what something *means* to a person and you have changed that person. This works more readily, and to better effect, for you than for anyone else. Similarly, change the routine activities in an organization, and you have changed the organization.

Growth, or Stagnation?

People who are not growing are stagnating. In much the same way, organizations that are not growing are stagnating.

Growth here means inventing new ways of solving old or persisting problems. If the same method of solving a problem is used two or three times, it becomes a habit. A habit enables you to deal with the world without thinking about it.

If the world were unchanging, this would work just fine. But the world is always changing. This makes it imperative that habits/routines be broken in order to engage the world by thinking about it rather than assuming it hasn't changed.

People who are stagnating and not growing are characterized by using yesterday's methods to deal with today's problems. The enemy of growth is smug self-satisfaction. The organizational equivalent is the *status quo* or bureaucracy—which amount to the same thing.

We have seen previously that

Learning = Growth, and that

Growth = Life.

Why anyone would want an organization that is not more alive is testimony to the power of habits of thought and of action. We also seem to assume that the alternative conditions can be created out of whole cloth.

They cannot be. Once the disease of the status quo or of bureaucracy has claimed it victims, the disease has to be "killed" by a more powerful agent than the one that permitted it to infect the organization. Habits cannot be talked out of existence. They have to be destroyed. They have to be displaced by other habits. If people are not thinking about what they are doing—or how they are doing it—the habits of thinking and engaging oneself must displace the habit of not doing so.

What doesn't grow, stagnates.

The Learning *Mode*

We have alluded to this off and on throughout this book. It is the ultimate key to the making of a competent organization.

Arie de Geus, who was head of planning for Royal Dutch Shell, stated the issue very concisely. This is what he concluded after a study of companies that have lasted the longest:

> *"The ability to learn faster than competitors may be the only sustainable advantage."*

We already know that organizations *per se* do not "learn." *Organization* is an abstraction. It is only people who can learn—or not.

So it comes down to two things:

- How fast the people who comprise the organization *can* learn; and

- How fast they can change the systems that either facilitate or impede their learning and their doing.

Learning is either a habit or a parlor game (often played in schools). You memorize something to pass a paper-and-pencil test and then it is soon forgotten. What is "learned" in classrooms is soon forgotten—roughly 95% in less than a year.

We seem dumb to the fact that there is no paper-and-pencil test in real life in a real world. We don't learn how to live in that real world. We learn only how to live and survive in the academic world.

A few people can learn in school, but only if they own their learning. Otherwise, learning for the real world only commences after people are confronted by it. Knowledge (making mental archives) is useful only if it contributes to your competency at life or at work. Judging from how many high school and college graduates seem unable to cope with the real world, apparently precious little of what we learn in school does.

Graduation is sometimes referred to as "Commencement." It is now time to start learning. The purpose of schooling should be to learn how to learn. The "game" is how many factoids you can remember until test time.

So we need a far better handle on the concept of learning even to understand what de Geus is saying. Any substantial learning is about the growth of the mind. And that growth is about mental arrangements that facilitate our navigation of the life and the purposes for it we have chosen. Otherwise it is useful only for quiz shows and for gossip and for one-upmanship in meetings.

So learning on the part of people in organizations is a matter of learning how to perform their roles better tomorrow than they did today, and how to design systems of work that facilitate and do not constrain their performance. It's not about the stock market (unless that is your unique role in the organization). It is not about current events (unless you have that designated surveillance responsibility).

It is about what you *need to know* or what you need to be able to do to perform your role better today than you did yesterday.

This is what de Geus meant by what he wrote. He didn't mean "training." He didn't mean accumulating experience. He meant being able to learn more that is pertinent to the performance of the people and the systems involved—and thus pertinent to the performance of the organization. It is about how fast people are growing and thus about how fast the organization is growing in capability or competence.

How will you know?

The best way to know is by measuring people's performance in their roles. If that is growing at the right (superior) pace, you can assume that learning is occurring. But if you want to know how to make learning *necessary*—how to instigate it and how to measure it, you may want to consider a tool for doing so.

This is a crude tool. There is no way to get precision about the learning required for continuously-elevated performance.

Evaluate yourself first. Then do so for all the people who report to you. Substitute their names for the "you" in the following.

Then have them evaluate themselves and compare yours with theirs—great basis for a productive discussion.

DO NOT use this as a part of any performance "appraisal." It is not about performance. It is about the main thing that drives performance. Use your assessment for your own purposes. Make your subjective assessment of others as a way of mentoring them. Otherwise, it is totally confidential between the two of you. It is for instilling or for raising your own or the other's learning mode.

Learning Mode Assessment Tool

Make your best judgment about each item. Use a scale of
1-10, 1 being "not much," and 10 being "to an impressive degree."

1. You have an insatiable curiosity about anything that bears or
    might bear on your performance, upstream or downstream
    in the organization, or outside the organization.
    Score: . . . .

2. You have an insatiable curiosity about how the systems
    in which you perform may facilitate or constrain your
    performance, and what you might do about that.
    Score: . . . .

3. You have an insatiable curiosity about the industry you
    work in, about where it came from and where it is going,
    and about how you might make it better.
    Score: . . . .

4. You seek out tougher and more challenging problems and
    responsibilities. You relish learning how to do something
    you have never done before.
    Score: . . . .

5. You are willing to risk failure, knowing that you can
    learn more from your failures than from your successes.
    Score: . . . .

6. Problems stimulate you, especially ones that you have
    not faced before.
    Score: . . . .

7. You love to find and study anything that might help you
    to perform better to morrow than you did today.
    Score: . . . .

8. You have boundless passion for your work and your role, as evidenced by the number and the quality of the questions you ask.
   Score: . . . .

9. You know who you want to be when you grow up, because you have done so. You believe deeply that you are the creator of your own destiny.
   Score: . . . .

10. You are ruthless about your own ROA.
    Score: . . . .

11. What you like most about other people and what you read is that they see the world differently than you do.
    Score: . . . .

12. You are totally committed to becoming more competent in your role, every day.
    Score: . . . .

13. You are competitively accomplish-minded and entrepreneurially-spirited. You are open to the world and engage it at every opportunity.
    Score: . . . .

You may want to add more. But these will cover the essentials. You may want to change the wording. Since these are private, you and those you mentor can be truthful. Otherwise, you are only deceiving yourself and wasting your time.

Problems and Accomplishments

Problems are what stand between you and what you intend to accomplish. You don't want to rid yourself of them—especially if you have not encountered them before. They can propel your learning.

Embrace them and learn what they have to teach. Expect everyone else to do the same.

A competent organization is not a problem-free organization. To the contrary, it is an organization that faces tougher and tougher problems. If you are trying to accomplish something, you will draw problems to your path. If you are trying to accomplish something that is truly great and worthy, the toughest problems will be on that path.

If you do not intend to accomplish anything special, then your problems will be no more than the conventional and the popular ones. If your organization has the same problems as most other organizations, you can readily deduce that you are not trying to accomplish anything beyond the ordinary.

It is by being ordinary and without purpose that most people—and most organizations—avoid having tougher problems than they are capable of dealing with.

Problems and obstacles and distractions come with the territory. If you are committed to accomplishing something truly bold and unique, they will arise to test your commitment. It is then that the lessons they hold for you can be revealed.

In other words, problems are to learn from. Pursuing your cause with passion and determination will bring them on in full force.

Here's the tool: If you are irretrievably in the learning mode, they are your teachers. If you are not, they are anathema to you. Which—you or your problems—will win out depends upon how competent you are, and how determined you are to achieve your purposes.

This is the case for individuals. This is therefore also the case for organizations.

Competent organizations—like competent people—are resilient. They may be temporarily stymied. But they will not be beat. That's what being competent means.

"Integrity"

Competent organizations—like competent people—have *integrity*. That is, they have no weaknesses that will bring down the whole.

They are competent through and through. That's real integrity. They "say" what they mean and they mean what they say. You can depend on them to do the right thing.

The *tool* here amounts to testing the organization every day (and in every way) for integrity. It means putting yourself in the place of every kind of user and every stakeholder to challenge the organization from their point of view.

A good analogy here is what the Navy means by the *integrity* of an ocean-going vessel. It means essentially that the vessel is "shipshape"—ready to go to sea and survive whatever it encounters. A person has integrity if they cannot be blown off course by the events of the day. An organization has integrity if every part of it is competent, thus adding up to a "shipshape" organization, capable of handling whatever comes its way. It has no weaknesses that could threaten the existence of the whole.

That kind of integrity is necessary if your organization is going to be fully competent.

Followership

We don't hear much about that these days. It seems that everyone wants to be the "leader."

The film *The Remains of the Day* reveals the critical importance—even the indispensability—of those who serve. It raises poignantly the respect due to subordinates who are masterful in their roles and have chosen to serve as a way of life.

We live in culture that is disdainful of masterful performance in the menial tasks of life. We consider ourselves above all that. We wouldn't survive without those who perform those menial tasks. We just want to appear to be superior. The only sense of duty we seem to have in America is what we owe ourselves. As the television commercial repeats over and over again—"We're worth it." Meaning, one supposes, that we are due whatever we want.

A competent organization cannot be made out of such attitudes. Someone has to sharpen the pencils. Someone has to sweep the floor.

Someone has to be serving as followers if there are to *be* "leaders." If they cannot do so with dignity and a clear-cut sense of relevance, neither can the "leader."

Those who are chosen to attend West Point are exposed to four full years of learning how to be followers. Why? Because it is well-known that the best leaders almost always come from the ranks of the best followers. It is only a person who knows how to contribute to the success of others who knows how to best lead others.

For these and other reasons, every organization that intends to be competent needs a "followership" program. In the trades, this is done via an apprenticeship. We would do well to bring that old-fashioned idea back. It is far superior to further years of education. There are things that cannot be taught. They can only be learned.

What needs to be learned about leadership can best be learned by serving, as a competent follower, a worthy and competent leader. Why can't we "get" this? The *logic* is irrefutable.

To design a potent "followership" program (probably needs to be referred to as "leadership development," because of our cultural anathema to "followership"), you would *minimally* want to consider the perspectives in the following:

> Rosanne Badowski, *Managing Up: How to Forge an Effective Relationship with Those above You*
> Stanley Bing, *Throwing the Elephant: Zen and the Art of Managing Up*
> Ira Chaleff, *The Courageous Follower: Standing Up to and for Our Leaders*
> Robert Kelley, *The Power of Followership*
> Michael Useem, *Leading Up: How to Lead Your Boss So You Both Win*

For every book about followership, there are probably 5,000 books about leadership. Don't let that fool you. Followership is more important in the most important ways.

THE COMPETENT ORGANIZATION

Indoctrination and Mentoring

Incoming people must learn the culture of the organization. If they are introduced to the organization's culture at the outset, that will speed along their learning period. This indoctrination period can serve two other purposes:

1. Require different top-level persons to run these indoctrination sessions and/or to speak at them. That will serve to remind them of the salient issues that people (including them) may need to learn about the organization's culture. It will also serve to sensitize them to the kinds of questions newcomers may continue to have about the organization and how it works.

2. Getting involved may reveal flaws in the organization's culture. There may be a discrepancy between what is said about the culture and what the culture is really like. Then one or the other have to be fixed.

If you are one of the leaders of the organization, you could learn a lot by sitting in and asking questions.

Members of the organization who have been on board for a while should also sit in on these sessions. You cannot remind people too often what the organization is **for**, and what its guiding values and beliefs are (or should be).

One of the best ways for existing members of the organization to learn better how the organization works is to teach it. Part of their continuous learning and development should involve their teaching different components of the indoctrination sessions.

Every newcomer to and every ongoing member of the organization should be assigned a **mentor**. The purpose of a mentor is not to help the mentee learn the technical aspects of his or her role. It is to guide that person in the direction of becoming a steward of the organization's cause in life. There are attitudes, there are ideologies, and there are mental models that can retard the performance of the organization. It is the mentor's role to detect these and to influence the mentee in a better direction.

Bosses are not *ipso facto* good mentors. This is something that has to be learned to be performed well. It may actually be advantageous for newcomers and ongoing members alike to have as a mentor a person other than their boss.

You should have an ongoing "school" where mentors can learn how to perform that role competently. Mentoring sessions should be largely Q&A sessions.

- It is only when mentors can lead themselves and others to valuable insights into what is going on (or not) that they are of value to mentees and to the organization.
- It is only when mentees provide the questions that constitute the agenda for mentoring sessions that they are win-win.

Mentors are not teachers. Their purpose is to help the mentee learn and grow. So they must also be learners. It is their curiosity about how to be helpful to each different mentee that can lead them to be better learners themselves.

There can be no one-size-fits-all mentoring program. It cannot be had off the shelf. You are different, your people are different, the circumstances are different, and your culture is different.

But people can be made into superior mentors if they know how to ask the right questions. And people can be led into being better mentees if they are in the learning mode and know how to ask the right questions.

The qualifications for being a great mentor are these:

- Your gratification in life come from seeing others you have helped become superior human beings and more competent mentors themselves.
- You are irretrievably in the learning mode. You have an insatiable curiosity about what bears upon people's performance at work and their hopes and dreams in general. You don't go in knowing this. You are there to produce insights.
- You have an insatiable curiosity about the mentor-mentee relationship and study it assiduously.

- You have a role in an organization whose culture recognizes mentoring as a skill set that is equivalent to any leadership skill set.
- You are yourself especially competent in your role, and you know what it takes to weather the ups and downs of learning how to perform one's role better tomorrow than yesterday.
- You have been recognized as an outstanding steward of "Mother's" (the organization's) health and welfare in your regular role.
- You have authored or co-authored your organization's manual for effective mentoring. You have made invited presentations on effective mentoring at professional conferences or in other organizations.
- You know how to mentor yourself, and you have the measurable results to prove it.

There may be other criteria. But these will help you to think about what's required and what's at stake.

Learning and Growth

It must be an absolute requirement in your organization for anyone who has a role in it to achieve "Mastery" in his or her role. This would be the number one bullet on everyone's Learning Plan.

"Mastery" in one's role means:

- You have mastered all aspects of your role, and are still improving your performance.
- You know what bears upon your performance, both within the organization upstream and downstream and externally.
- You know how to prevent problems, you know how to anticipate problems you can't prevent, and you know how to solve most problems that come your way in the performance of your role.
- You could masterfully teach your role to another person,
- You understand how your organization works—operationally and economically.
- You know who your competitors are and how they work.
- You are totally familiar with your industry and its history, as well as the history of your own organization,

- You know what it costs to provide you with the infrastructure and the support you need to perform your role, and you know how to do more with less.
- You know as much as your "boss" knows about how to manage your part of the organization, and would be able to do so.
- You are an innovator in your role.
- You have recruited one or two great performers to the organization.
- You are capable of representing your company in front of its customers or other stakeholders.

Having a level or two of learning/performance above the achievement of "Mastery" is helpful. For example, the first mastery level might be identified as Mastery 3rd class, the next level of achievement in role would be Mastery 2nd class, and the top level Mastery 1st class. The terminology for these distinctions is not important. But having ways to recognize continuous learning and growth in performance is.

This can be done in any department of the organization—from Accounting to IT to Engineering and H/R.

Having achievement ranks for the managers who report to you can also be useful. In the typical organization, people come to work in that organization and work at what they consider a dead-end "job" from then on. People need to see some benefit from growing more competent in the role they have in the organization.

Their performance needs to be measured and they need to have some way of moving up except promotion. The level of performance in role is often more valuable to the organization than merely moving someone up the corporate ladder to start again in a role they have not mastered.

It is growth in competence within roles that matters most. Measure it and recognize it in this or some other way.

In his book, Talent Is Overrated, *Geoffrey Colvin cited research which showed clearly that simply performing an activity for a long period of time is no guarantee that people will get better at it, and sometimes they get worse.*

17. Still More Tools and Techniques

Over the years, I have partnered with a great many CEOs to engineer and develop high-performance organizations. Together, we invented a wide range of "pushes" and "pulls" as tools for making their organizations sustainably more competent. These were often quite different organizations in different industries, including banks and retail, manufacturing firms, service and engineering organizations, government agencies, not-for-profits, and the military.

Those tools and techniques were custom-designed for a particular organization, as they must be. What's being offered here is a sampling of some of the tools and techniques that could be of use in any type of organization.

Communication Rules of the Road

When any kind of traffic increases to fill the pathways available, rules of the road had to be created to enable the traffic to flow more efficaciously.
This has been the case on land, on the sea, and in the air. Commercial and private planes have to fly a specified route at a specified altitude, in order to accommodate the huge increases there have been.

Although the media used may have changed due to technological advances, communication remains the "nervous system" of any organization. People have to communicate with one another if they are to get any kind of collaborative work done.

Let us review the situation:

- There is now a surfeit, an overload even, of communication in every sort of organization.
- "Information" seems to expand to fill the capacity of the storage or distribution technologies, not the need to know, and have thus become heavily irrelevant, and thus more of a hindrance than a help.

All robustly-competent organizations have devised communication "Rules of the Road." When anyone can talk to anyone else at will, there is a lot of noise in every channel, if not raw chaos. So, like all transport systems, there must be some imposed rules and regulations.

Part of the solution to the communication problem in organizations is not *more* communication, but less. In most cases, there is already too much.

For example, when anyone gets a phone call, he or she is required to ask up front, "Please tell me what you are trying to accomplish by this call, and I will help you." Often the caller can't really articulate the desired accomplishment. So the staffer leads the way to arriving at a specific accomplishment, and then the collaboration needed to get there.

Similarly, every one in the organization who uses the phone is required to zero in on a specific accomplishment before they pick up the phone.

In most contemporary organizations, email is as much abused as it is overused.

- As is the case with the telephone, people typically don't think through what they intend to accomplish, or how.
- It is a lazy person's tool. It is too easy to use and it is too easy to network other people. Just press a button.
- It is speed on drugs. People neither compose emails thoughtfully nor read them thoughtfully. After a while, their minds atrophy. They just go through the motions. It is an activity. People are the "droids" for the power of the technology.

There need to be clear rules of the road for the use of such a potent medium. I once advised a CEO client that his in-box clutter was his own fault. So we devised a rule. He sent a memo to all of those who regularly addressed him: "If you once more send me an email which contains information I don't need to know, you can no longer address me by email." Period.

That worked so well that we invented a further item for the rules of the road. If anyone sent or received an email which was not strategically pertinent to the addressees' performance at work, they were placed on probation. If they became routine abusers, their email privileges were taken away from them.

Furthermore, if they sent or received more than 10 emails a day from within the organization, they had to justify that abuse in front of a "traffic cop." That's the person who uses the equivalent of "radar" to keep an eye on what's going on, and why.

People typically do not strategize their selection of the media they use. In competent organizations, they are required to do so. There are always better media requiring better preparation. Competent people waste neither their own time and attention nor that of those they engage in communication.

"Strings" are easy. In competent organizations, people don't use strings. They are required to summarize the situation to date and start anew.

And so on. Whatever irritates users, or whatever does not contribute to the performance of the organization, is where there needs to be a rule as a part of the communication "rules of the road" which everyone must adhere to.

Before we take our leave of communication concerns once again, we should remind ourselves of the relationship between communication and *performance*:

- *Talk is talk and performance is performance.*
- *Except for those rare individuals who say what they mean, and mean what they say, there is no necessary correlation between what people say and what they do.*
- *Therefore, measure performance only by performance, not by talk about performance. People's statements about their experiences or their credentials is talk **about** (past) performance. The only performance that really counts is what they increasingly contribute to the organization's health and welfare in their roles.*

- *Talk is cheap, whatever the medium employed. But performance has to be achieved through diligent and continuous growth over time.*
- *The **only** measure of performance is performance.*

Invent the Problems You Need

The more incompetent the organization, the more likely it is that it will be *passively* buffeted by the problems of the day. Unlike conventional organizations, the most competent ones will by their decisions and actions actually *create* the problems they encounter.

Problems—like failures—are best used as sources of learning and growth in competence.

Henry Ford and Thomas Edison agreed, and it was Edison who said:

> *"Some of the best lessons we ever learn we learn from our mistakes and failures."*

And, we will add here, some of the best lessons for competent organizations come from working out solutions for the problems they have not encountered previously—solutions that do not simply solve the problem *per se*, but speed them on their path to their chosen purposes.

As paradoxical as it may seem, if you *choose* the problems you need to learn from and grow on, you will readily surpass others on the same journey. When you choose your purposes and dedicate yourself to them, you will bring upon yourself the problems that occur when you are striving.

The earliest climbers of the world's tallest mountains set their sights on the summit. The problems they encountered had to do with getting there. This is what is meant by *choosing* the problems you need to deal with.

They had to face the problems that came with their commitment to reach the summit.

Job Shops vs. Assembly Lines

- Do not attempt to apply the process of the repetitive operations of assembly lines if you have a job shop.
- Do not try to apply the logic of the unique operations of a job shop if you have assembly line repetitive operations.

They are incompatible.

If you have ever waited in line for your turn in an "Emergency Room," you will have experienced the attempt to use assembly line logic in a job shop. "Education" is essentially an assembly line operation. If we designed an organization for "Learning," it would function more like a job shop. Libraries are job shops. For the most part, they do not work well from the customer's perspective—as *efficient* as they may be for the staff.

Being on hold ("Your call is very important to us") is a function of the software available. It is not very effective from the customer's or client's point of view.

The invention of the assembly line was a huge step forward in the production of automobiles. That philosophy came to dominate thinking about designing the operation of all kinds of organizations from the early 20th-century to the present time.

But people are not automobiles. They are not put together in the same way. And they do not function in the same way.

The criteria applied in a love affair are not about production or about efficiency.

Whenever the efficiency of the organization interacts negatively with the efficiency of the user, there is a problem. And the underlying problem may well be that of trying to apply job shop mentality to continuous assembly line mentality—or vice versa.

The "tool" here is that of determining what kind of mentality the user expects, and designing the organization to fit *those* expectations. Just because there is software that seduces you in the other direction doesn't satisfy the interface. We have gained much in the making of inanimate objects using the logic of the assembly line and of supply chains.

That thinking applied to other kinds of uses has served us ill. People don't go to a bookstore to find something of value to read. They go there to be told what others are reading, because that criterion is applied to you. How things are done affects *human nature*. Do you know any computer programmers who lie awake at night worrying about *that*?

The genius behind the evolution of Amazon.com was how to run a job shop for whatever requests or questions came their way.

Should grocery stores be more like that? Or merely for distribution?

Solutions in Search of a Problem

This is a useful way of defining people in conventional organizations. They are like the proverbial hammer running around looking for a nail to pound on.

They are like bundles of solutions scanning the environment for a problem to pounce on. Some physicians—and other experts—are that way. It many cases, it is a solution that actually *creates* the problem.

Competent organizations do not function in this way. They know that observing things without the burden of preconceptions enables the observer to see what's there rather than what they *expected* to be there. They see every new situation with fresh and uncontaminated eyes.

Competent organizations are more innovative. They invent a way forward. They are not constrained by rote ways of looking at problems and circumstances.

There may be a certain *efficiency* in applying past mental models to present circumstances. There is little *efficacy* in doing so. Just because something worked in the past is no guarantee that it will work in the present or the future. Circumstances are always changing. People who are not open to those changes will not see how present circumstances differ from past circumstances. They will be looking for what's similar or the "same" as when they were previously "successful."

Competent people—and competent organizations—let reality light the way ahead, not their own predilections or experiences from the past.

The advantages can be enormous.

Hindsight/Foresight

> *"If a man's foresight was as good as his hindsight, he'd be better off by a damn sight."*
> —Columnist Evan Esar

What competent organizations know that less competent organizations don't seem to know is that the future hasn't happened yet. You can't "see" something that hasn't happened yet—except in your imagination. So it isn't so much a matter of prescience as it is a matter of *how* you imagine it.

Esar's clever comment (above) is provocative, as far as it goes. But it doesn't go far enough.

Here's a better take on the issues involved:

- Hindsight is far from being 20/20. The past is as much an interpretation as is the present. We don't see or remember the world as it *is*. We see it or remember it as we *interpret* it.
- We make a story out of the present to fit our interpretations of it. We do the same with the past. The past is a story we concoct to accommodate what we take to be the "facts."
- Our hindsight is thus as much a fiction as the future is. We interpret the future in terms of our hopes and fears about it. That permits us to tell the story of the future by extrapolating it out of our interpretations of our present and our past.
- Competent people—and competent organizations—take advantage of this very human predicament. They don't predict the future, which no one can. Nor do they wait passively for the future to

happen to them. As the very reliable saying goes, "The best way to predict the future is to invent it."
- That's what competent people—and competent organizations—do.

No future can be invented out of whole cloth. Like it or not, it has to be invented out of present circumstances—the realities of the present. The most remarkable leaders have been like alchemists. They start with the same present that others have, but make of that far more than others seem to be capable of.

Every race is won or lost on the same track. Every boxing match is won or lost in the same ring. Every marriage is made by the people involved. Every organization's future—to the extent it *can* be "invented"—is invented in the same circumstances as other organizations exist in.

The difference, therefore, has to be what is uniquely capable for that organization given how it is composed, its culture, and the competence of its people.

It is only competent people—and competent organizations—that are able to invent their futures within the constraints of the real world which envelop all organizations and their people. The difference lies in how competent they are to invent the future—and the future circumstances—they need to achieve their purposes in that future.

Hindsight and foresight are both overrated. They both can make us suffer by being overly-rational. What is underrated is the competence required to invent the future and then to make it come about.

The title of Melvin Konner's 1990 book is *Why the Reckless Survive.* It is about risk-taking. This is what competent organizations—like competent people—are willing to do: take risks. They take risks less competent people and organizations will not.

To take risks means to take the risk of failure. It isn't failure that is rewarded in competent organizations. It is risk-taking. There is no safe journey to excellence. It requires taking risks.

Only those who risk the future gain the right to claim it. That world belongs to the bold. The more competent the person—or the organization—the bolder they can function.

Hindsight and foresight are both bugbears of the timid and the incompetent. The world belongs not to them but to those who make it.

All others are trapped in a squirrel cage of words.

Project Management

Every human endeavor is a "project," as is every encounter. The receptionist who answers the phone is entering into a project. The sales call is a project. In a restaurant, the waitperson's engagement with his or her customers is a project. The roles we undertake at work or in society can all be seen as projects. The case could be made that life itself is an ongoing "project." Certainly the life and destiny of every organization is a project.

Yet there are very few people who are competent at *managing* projects— including those who have had formal training in doing so.

Because we don't see what we are doing when we enter into a conversation with someone—or read a book—as a "project," it doesn't occur to us to take advantage of some of the best methods of project management.

As a result, our meetings are not as productive as they could be. Our conversations are not as useful as they could be. The performance of the organization is often not what it could be, or should be. We don't see "getting things done right" as a project—and hence the right things don't always get done. Or, if they do, they don't get done in the right way.

Competent people are by definition project managers. They equip themselves and manage themselves in order to accomplish what needs accomplishing. The more competent its people, the more competent the organization is.

Here is what you need to do about this:

- If you have less-than-competent people, you must put them in a system that makes possible what they need to do, and at the same time makes it *necessary*. You can make the system be the "manager" of the projects undertaken.

- You don't need a "manager" if you can devise a system that manages the work and the outcomes.

- A project team requires competent people. If they are competent enough, they will effectively "manage" the work to be done to achieve the results intended—in their interactions with one another.

- You have only two choices with incompetent people:

  1. Make them competent; or
  2. Make them leave.

  Poor leaders seem to assume that there is a third or fourth choice. If you intend to have a competent organization, there are no alternatives that are effective. Incompetent people are not even very good at following directions or procedures. And, as noted earlier, if it takes two people (e.g., the person and the boss) to perform one role costs go up disproportionately.

- Everyone in a project team should be capable of managing the team. There should be no people involved who need to be "managed."

If you need to do some training (or further development) in project management, a splendid one-book resource would be

Jerry Manas, *Napoleon on Project Management*

Many of the world's great modern leaders (Patton, for example) have studied Napoleon's methods to their advantage.

Just don't fall into the trap of assuming that projects and project teams have to be "managed" in the conventional way.

THE COMPETENT ORGANIZATION

The more rote the thinking, the more obstacles to performance there will be. Competent people know when—and how—to improvise, which is always the ultimate principle, beyond Napoleon's six.

Power and Influence

Both influence and power are addictive. You need them both. The problem is how to avoid becoming addicted to them.

The best use of power is the least use—no more than is absolutely necessary. People are attracted to powerful people. They just don't want the power used arbitrarily on *them*.

Power is not divisible. You cannot "empower" other people by giving them some of yours. Power is in the eye of the beholder. It is not a commodity. Theodore Roosevelt's "Walk softly but carry a big stick" is a pertinent aphorism. The power you don't use is what makes you powerful in others' eyes. The more of it you believe you have to use, the less you will have.

Power is always tacit—always understood. The less you wield, the more you will have. Character is what you have in reserve.

You will influence people whether you intend to or not. If nothing else, you have position power, the power that comes with your position in the scheme of things. You must be at all times aware of this. You want only to influence people to become more competent, to become the masters of their own destiny, and to become indispensable stewards of the organization's mission. Any egoistic use of influence detracts from what it should be used for.

*Influence yourself to become more competent daily in your role as leader. Then let who you **are** do the influencing of others. If you are who you should be, that kind of influence will be sufficient.*

All anyone else is capable of seeing is your performance in your role.

They cannot see who you "are." So let your performance do the talking.

Through your influence over others, help them to become more like you are—or, better, to become more like they should become.

Care about the person that they *should* be and could be. That might influence them to *become* that person. That is your task. Make it possible, and make it necessary. That is the best use of **influence.**

Accountability and Relevance

People are relevant to the organization to the extent that they are accountable for their performance in their roles.

In the average organization, people feel less relevant to the project that *is* the organization. So they typically report dissatisfaction with their jobs. Again, however, it is a matter of how competent they are in their roles. The more competent they are, the more relevant they feel and the happier they are in their work.

So there are two underlying problems:

1. One is that people's performance is not well measured, or measured at all; and
2. The other is that people are not expected (or it is not necessary) to become more competent in their roles over time.

It is not perfect, but the best tool that we have developed for these two problems is what we have called the **Appreciated Value Index.**

The "appreciated" means that people are expected to *increase* their value to the organization over time. The "index" means that everyone starts with a nominal index of 100. Then, depending upon what they accomplish that testifies to their value to the organization, their index can rise or fall.

The criteria for measurement are set forth below. This makes possible a rank ordering of the "most valuable players" in the organization for each period of time—say a year. We have also used this index as a very effective and highly superior way of determining salary increases and/or bonuses.

To repeat, this way of measurement is not perfect. But (a) it is far better than no measurement at all, and (b) you may think of criteria that are more valid for your particular purposes. What the index loses in validity, it gains in reliability. That is, it will reveal positive or negative changes over time—which is what you need to assess performance and thus confer relevance on the people in your organization.

There are two assumptions here that deserve your particular attention:

- One is that every person will need to become familiar with the economics of the firm.
- The other is that the person would be able to calculate (roughly) how his or her own P&L statement would contribute to the whole.

It is possible, with the help of very creative financial people, to create these P&L statements for every employee in the organization, from the CEO on down. That would go beyond the reach of this present book. Just know that it is doable, and has been done.

Here are some measurement criteria for an "Appreciated Value Index." The weight that you would give each item depends upon what kind of particular "pushes" and "pulls" you want to establish in your organization.

Key Factors to Consider in Developing an Appreciated Value Index

- *Contribution: What the individual contributes to the "Bottom Line." That is, the dollar value of his or her contribution to the economic circumstances of the organization. This is difficult, but possible, to assess.*

- *Costs: Most organizations simply don't know what their costs are per employee. The know what their "labor" costs are, what their capital and other aggregated costs are, what their "overhead" or undistributed burden costs are, etc. But they cannot run even a crude P&L on individual employees (including the executives). What you're after here is total costs vs. total contribution—each employee's marginal contribution. Employees consume organizational resources differentially. What do they cost in terms of direct support, or back office support? Sales people and IT people consume inordinate amounts* *of resources. What you want to know, essentially, is what the **burden absorption** rate per each employee is. That is a very valuable number even if it is crude. If your present accountants and/or finance people are not clever enough to figure out how to distribute operating costs according to actual consumption of those costs, simply consider the total operating costs, and distribute the burden to people according to their salaries or some other measure. The point is that it should technically be possible to reduce the organization's burden or overhead to zero by apportioning those costs ideally to individual employees, or minimally to specific departments.*

- *Quality: Service people and retail clerks—every employee, including the CEO—should also be measured in terms of quality. These may be measures of efficiency or effectiveness, or the costs of errors, mistakes, or lack of competent engagement, or the costs of meetings and other communication vs. the consequences. Again, a measure somewhat unconventional and therefore difficult to measure, but worth the effort.*

- *Process or product improvement ideas, implemented: The number of such improvements plus their dollar value, factored in some way that makes sense and has the right pushes and pulls. For the CEO, this might have to be marginal contribution plus the value of such things as acquisitions, organizational changes, meetings, etc. Include here new sources of revenue minus costs.*

- *Safety and/or health (of the organization) ideas: Those of significant and measurable consequence: number plus dollar value.*

- *New members: recruiting and sponsorship of new members whose AVIs outpace the average. Plus track record as a "talent scout."*

- *Involvements and accomplishments that enhance the reputation of the organization amongst stakeholders, including customers, suppliers, and employees.*

- *"Assists": Measurable contributions to the capabilities and the performance of peers and associates, up, down, and around.*

- *Leadership: Measurable improvement in knowing when to lead, when to follow, and when to get out of the way.*

The primary value of this tool lies in the discussions required to implement it. The validity of the AVI is secondary. It reliability—that is, its ability to measure changes over time—is its real value.

This is not intended to be an exhaustive or exclusive list. It is meant only to suggest some basic ways of calculating the increased or decreased value to every employee to the organization over time. You may want to add or modify the measures used.

The AVI, along with the measurement of performance improvement you can get from the role description process will provide you what you need to have a good sense of the growth of the competence of the organization from the inside-out.

". . . it is only by working at what you can't do that you turn into the expert you want to become."

— K. Anders Ericsson

18. Practice, Preparedness, Purpose, Perseverance, Possibility

It has been a bit of a fashion in recent years to talk about perfecting one's strengths. Weaknesses were presumed not to matter nearly as much.

So the notion of "practicing" is at once a controversial one, and one which is not much practiced within organizations.

> There is the old saw about the driver who stopped at a street corner in NYC to ask a person carrying a violin case how to get to Carnegie Hall. The person's response was, "Practice, practice, practice."

If that is what works for athletes and for musicians and for artists and actors, why wouldn't it be a prerequisite for organizations that intend to become masterful at what they do?

- The primary reason seems to be that, unlike the military and sports, etc., the organization once created is always fully engaged in its business. There is precious little time for practicing. We are always up against just "doing it."
- Another reason is just as constraining, but even stranger. It is the belief that once a person is marginally capable of doing something, all the rest of becoming really good at it can be learned "on the job." No professional golfer or basketball player would assume that they could break records solely by learning while on the job.

- Yet another reason may be that people look at business organizations particularly as places where "amateurs" can succeed. The Broadway show was entitled "How to Succeed in Business without Really Trying." Andrew Keen entitled his book on the contemporary culture "The Cult of the Amateur."
- It seems further to be assumed that people are "human resources," and are thus relatively interchangeable. So why would a person want to devote the time and effort required to become really, really good at what he or she does?

One thing is certain. We may invest billions of dollars in "training." But we do not see much in the way of *continuous* improvement in the performance of *every* role in our organizations and the performance of the organization as a whole. We have taken the wrong path. Employees are not pigeons, to be trained to jump at carrots or to avoid kicks in the butt.

It isn't occasional "training" that we need. It is continuous learning. That's what produces continuous improvement. To go from "good to great" requires being good. And what made your organization "good" is the same thing that will make it great—getting better every day at everything that is done in your organization.

The tools and techniques suggested here and in the preceding chapters will make significant contributions to the development of a fully competent organization. Don't be distracted by being "great." You can't magically leapfrog there. You first have to be fully competent.

Practice

It has long been known (apparently by all but our snake-oil gurus) that the only way to get better is by deliberate practice. The best-sellers reveal the "secrets" of greatness. Colin Powell says there are none. It's a matter of getting better and better at the basics. That's the path to the competent person—and the competent organization.

But "deliberate practice"? How is that going to happen in an organization that hasn't even enough time to carry out the urgent activities of the day?

When is a professional who is performing every minute of every day going to "practice"?

There are three good ways of solving this (apparent) problem:

- One is to take the position that what goes on everywhere every day IS practice. People (including the CEO) are practicing today to get better tomorrow at what they do. There is no "bottom line" to track the growth of the competence of people—or of the organization. There should be. If there were, we would pay far more and far better attention to it. Nothing complicated is required here. It is simply a matter of starting with today's baseline and then measuring for continuous improvement in the performance of every role, This is what pays off for the organization. You cannot make an organization competent merely through magic tricks performed by its "leaders."

- Another is for the CEO to be held responsible for the growth in learning and hence in the performance of his or her people. The best way of doing this is to confront those people with scenarios that are wholly unlike the routines of the day—of the status quo—and require them to think through a course of action. For example, the CEO may be talking to the COO and confronts him with this problem: "Suppose five of your best people go down together in a tragic accident. You are Mother's steward. What would you do? I'd like to see three well-thought-out and plausible responses by Friday. OK?" Another example: "Who is the best COO in our industry—or in any industry for that matter? Why is he or she better than you? What are you planning to do about it?" Examples abound. Require each person who reports to you to think through a situation that they have never encountered. It is by learning what we don't know, or doing what we can't do, that we learn. Require every "leader"—or every manager—to do the same continuously on an arbitrary schedule. *Do not let up.*

- Yet another is through the use of *simulation*. Airline pilots do not become more competent merely by flying. They are continuously exposed (as are astronauts, etc.) to virtual realities in simulators that they may never encounter—but *could* encounter. Competent people will of course do this for themselves with little or no prodding. But stasis is the enemy. And that sets in for everyone—including you. If a person is not growing in competency, they are shrinking in competency. The most elaborate and potent scheme I have ever seen for doing this is a whole organization simulation that we concocted for the organization of a client. This presented every member of the organization with a virtual world different from the one they worked in every day. And it changed by what was done within it on a daily basis—including what customers and suppliers did, and what the economy was doing, as well as the ever-advancing technology. They were required to play this "game" with the same dedication that they played the game of the actual business.

The very least that needs to be done is pushing and pulling the CEO out of his or her comfort zone by a coach or consultant. Then it requires doing this for every manager, and that manager for every person down the line. The aim is to enhance the thinking and thus the competence of every person's performance.

> *People who are not **practicing** to get better, won't.*

As the columnist and quipster Evan Esar put it, taking off from Shakespeare's analogy :

> *"All the world's a stage, and most of us need more rehearsals."*

As we shall see.

Preparedness

In American culture particularly, we have come to assume that "practicing" is sufficient. It is not. What's required is *deliberate practice*.

And that means practicing for some specific purpose. It means practicing to be prepared to fulfill some present or long-term purpose.

When the concert master walks onto the stage, he or she is fully prepared to perform their role flawlessly. The burger-flipper isn't. Does it make a difference in the performance of the orchestra or the fast-food restaurant?

The soldier who is ill-prepared is more likely to die, or to be an accessory to the death of his comrades. The parent who is not well-prepared for parenthood is more likely to produce children who fail society. The surgeon who is not well-prepared for the operation may make a mistake. The pupil who is not well-prepared for the class diminishes the value of the class for all of the other pupils. People who are not rightly prepared to live meaningful lives will live lives of relative meaninglessness. A person who is not prepared to learn cannot learn.

It helps—can there be any real argument here?—if you are going to climb Mount Everest or run the marathon or conduct the choir to be prepared to do so.

For our purposes here is the bottom line: The leader who is not prepared to lead will have an organization that is not prepared to perform. An organization that is fully prepared to perform can do so without the presence of a "leader." A great leader may *enhance* the performance of a fully-competent organization over time. But there never has been a great leader who could compensate for the lack of preparedness—either his or her own or the organization's lack of preparedness.

It is not enough just to "show up." If you are not fully prepared by the practicing you have engaged in, you are at best only half there.

Competent people have a mental checklist about their preparedness for the day or the endeavor: Are they personally prepared? Do they have the right resources? Have they practiced unforeseen events? Can they improvise? Do they know how to perform in such a way that they enable better and better performances by the others around them? Do they know exactly what their next steps will be after they have accomplished their purposes? What is their plan if for any reason they can't perform as required by the circumstances? And so on.

There is competence. And then there is preparedness. It takes both. Preparedness increases your competence. And your competence defines the breadth and the depth of the preparedness you need.

THE COMPETENT ORGANIZATION

It is not enough just to "be prepared" in some general sense. You must be *specifically prepared for doing what needs doing, and to accomplish what needs accomplishing.* This is the difference between the Special Forces (e.g., the Seals) and the main units of the military.

Being prepared means you are not betting on the competence developed in your "experience" alone. You are betting that nothing is capable of standing between you and your goal. You are prepared for whatever occurs along the way, even the unexpected.

There are two short quotations we can use to illumine the many-faceted idea of preparedness.

First, there is this comment from the famous scientist Louis Pasteur in 1854:

> *"Where observation is concerned, chance favors only the prepared mind."*

Prepare your mind for its tasks first. All the rest depends upon how prepared your mind is for the tasks it faces. The performance of the organization depends mainly upon the preparedness of the minds involved.

There is no preparation that matters more.

Then there is this to ponder from Ralph Waldo Emerson, in 1876:

> *"The right performance of this hour's duties will be the best preparation for the hours or ages that follow it."*

How well people perform their present duties is the best predictor of how prepared they are going to be for tomorrow's challenges. This thought reveals the cumulative nature of preparedness, and how it depends upon the level of performance that precedes present need. You can't turn preparedness on or off.

It is past performance that determines present preparedness. It is present performance that determines future preparedness.

How a person performs his or her present role is the source of their future preparedness. How an organization performs its multifarious tasks today will determine whether or not it is prepared for tomorrow.

Performance and preparedness are thus wholly interdependent. *You can't have the one without the other.*

Purpose

If performance does not advance your purpose, it merely serves as a kind of social lubricant—effective or not. If performance does not advance your purpose, it advances the problems that will befall you.

You can only prepare for a purpose. Your performance will take you along the track it makes. If it is not for some specific purpose, it will contribute to the meaninglessness of your performance.

These imperatives hold for your organization as well as for every individual in it—including you.

Having a purpose creates a panoply of meaningfulness in your life—as it does for the life of the organization. There is little meaning to be had in a life that has no purpose. There is a sort of meaninglessness or ambiguity in an organization that has no collective purpose. If the reasons for the *existence* of the organization are not a set of purposes that its members can subscribe to, it has no collective purpose. It is then merely a collection of people pursuing their own purposes (if indeed they have any of import).

To make a profit is not a purpose. That is merely a means to some end. To serve the society is not a purpose. To what end? To be competent is not a purpose. It is a means to some specific purpose. Having a competent organization may be a good thing. But unless there is a purpose for being competent, it has no direction.

It makes no sense to talk about competence without purpose. It makes no sense to talk about purpose without competence.

Each of these—competence and purpose—calls upon the other to realize some endeavor, to contribute in some significant and meaningful way to a better life, a better world. It is *that* kind of purpose that people can subscribe to. They ask: Why am *I* here? Why does this organization exist? What is it *for*? What am *I for* here within it?

These are the questions people want answered about purpose. The better you can answer them, the more they will be a part of the whole process—assuming a great and worthy purpose.

People want to belong to something that is bigger and more relevant than they are. The leader(s) must provide this "something." It is a daily answer to the question: "Why are we all here?"

A purpose is compelling so long as it is alive and well in the everyday activities and accomplishments of the members of the organization. If it is the engine of the culture, it fires performance. If it is not, it is merely words.

What *purpose* should mean to leaders is well put by George Bernard Shaw (in the *epistle dedicatory* to his 1903 play *Man and Superman*):

> "This is the true joy in life, the being used for a purpose recognized by yourself as a mighty one; the being thoroughly worn out before you are thrown on the scrap heap; the being a force of nature instead of a feverish selfish little clod of ailments and grievances complaining that the world will not devote itself to making you happy."

It is the right message for those who entertain the thought that they have a purpose.

Note first that it is being *had by* your purpose that matters—not merely "having" one. What you "have" you can abandon. What has you, you cannot.

Second, note the phrase "being a force of nature." A force of nature is irresistible. It is indefatigable. It has its way with the world. It is not, itself, to be had. It is to be dealt with because there is no option. Great leaders must first deal with themselves. This enables them to require that others deal with them.

And this in turn leads to our next consideration . . . .

Perseverance

You may be had by your purpose. You may have all of the skills required. But you may sometimes encounter the kind of resistances that demand your perseverance. Sometimes perseverance wins when all else fails.

For a fully competent organization, people must persevere in their learning and therefore improved performance—forever. That's what perseverance requires. There is no final goal. People must persevere in becoming better today than they were yesterday in their roles. That is a chief distinction of competence.

Perseverance does not arise from extra effort. Perseverance is implicit in the GBS quotation above. It comes from irresistible determination. And that is a bundle of habits. Perseverance is not an act. It is a habit.

If you want a competent organization, you must do whatever it takes every day, without respite. It is when people have no option but to get better every day in their roles that most will do so. What's inherent in the culture of the competent organization is that necessity—it continues its influence no matter what this or that individual says to challenge it.

When a critical mass of the people in an organization are committed to the organization's mission in life, others may complain. But they will either escape or acquiesce. That's what collective perseverance produces.

The leader's perseverance is indispensable. But it is not enough where an organization or a society are concerned. The leader must have a power base—of incorrigible stewards of the organization's mission, of a potent organizational culture, of local celebrity—to ensure success. Perseverance without a great and worthy purpose is madness. Perseverance without the power to make things happen, without the power to make them "stick," is mere obstinacy.

Samuel Adams coupled *fortitude* and *perseverance* in a stirring speech in 1771. You cannot persevere without the fortitude to do so. These are characteristics of great leaders. They are therefore *habits*. Without the habits of fortitude and perseverance, you cannot be "a force of nature." Neither can your organization.

In *Rasselas* (1759), Samuel Johnson wrote—

"Great works are preformed not by strength but by perseverance."

Great works take time. Talent counts. Diligence counts. Competence counts. But the greater the work to be accomplished, the more important is perseverance.

Rome, as the old saying has it, was not built in a day. Today matters. But not as much as all the tomorrows that follow.

Possibility

All competent people are possibility thinkers. To use a current cliché, they are capable of "thinking outside the box." They can always imagine an alternative—alternative methods and alternative outcomes.

One philosopher referred to these as "alternities"—as alternative ways of imagining and perceiving the world. Those alternities produce a lived-in world that is different from what we would expect from our conventional wisdoms. They disrupt the evolution of things. They are thus vital for the creation and maintenance of a competent organization.

As the British physicist, engineer, and inventor Dennis Gabor wrote back in 1963 (in his book *Inventing the Future*):

"The future cannot be predicted, but it can be invented."

That future—for any organization as well as any society—can only be invented out of possibility thinking. What's possible?

Great leaders have always been the exemplars of possibility thinking. They are undeterred by the limits of conventional thinking. They get their minds "outside the box" and look around from that vantage point. Leaders—like the most competent thinkers of every stripe—do not dwell on what is said to be impossible. Their thinking is that whatever is impossible is merely a belief that has not been proven wrong.

Competent people—and competent organizations—take the impossible as a problem to be solved. Then they do what has to be done to make it possible (as Thomas Edison said).

What we forget is that it is all invented. Our present ways of viewing the world, individually or collectively, were invented. They become sacrosanct, as do all beliefs held by large numbers of people over time.

The competent person recognizes that we are on the wrong path. The jazz musician starts an improvisation that somehow just doesn't work. Does he or she ask the gods of music to change things so his improvisation does work? No. He or she changes the path they are on to get on a path that does work. An alternative might work. But it first has to be imagined, then tested while the band plays on.

The famous American poet Emily Dickinson wrote,

> *"I dwell in Possibility—*
> *A fairer House than Prose—*
> *. . . ."*

The prosaic in our lives constrains us. The prosaic is the status quo, the rules and mental models by which we live our lives. It is in imagining an alternative (and making it happen) that we invent a "fairer House" to live in.

What's "reasonable" has its uses. But it is what's possible that gives rise to a discontinuous way of doing things. It is the imaginative leap that makes the difference.

It was the philosopher Arthur Schopenhauer (19th-century) who wrote:

> *"Every man* [read every person] *takes the limits of his own field of vision for the limits of the world."*

THE COMPETENT ORGANIZATION

232

What we "see" when we look at the world is what we are capable of seeing, and what we expect to see. It is possibility thinking that sets a person—or an organization—free of those constraints.

As Dickinson put it, they "dwell in Possibility . . . ." They don't see the world in terms of right and wrong. They see the world in terms of the possibilities for inventing it. A problem is not an obstacle. It is an opportunity to re-invent the world in some small or large way. A failure is not a negative thing. It is an opportunity to re-invent the approach and go at it again.

The "bottom line" for competent people and competent organizations is not financial. It is a measure of how much possibility thinking is going on. The money appears in the wake of their ship. The more possibility thinking that goes on, the bigger the wake.

Possibility thinking is just as contagious as is conventional thinking. The more of it there is, the more of it there will be.

The same Dennis Gabor as above wrote these challenging lines:

> *"The more permissive the society, the less permissive must be the education which makes the individual fit to live in it."*

Every leader of every kind of organization needs to think hard about this.

What it says is that if your people came from permissive backgrounds, the less permissive your organization can be. You can't have a possibility-thinking culture unless you have people who are well-disciplined—who are fully competent. That's why the McDonald's kitchens work by timers and bells.

Benjamin Zander, co-author (with his wife Rosamund) of *The Art of Possibility*, is also conductor of the Boston Philharmonic Orchestra. He wants everyone in his orchestra to be first-chair. To make this possible, he knows that they must come prepared, having practiced many hours in advance of arriving. It is their discipline that enables them to be possibility thinkers.

If you want to build a competent organization, you have to start with competent people. People raised permissively are toxic to the possibility of a competent organization—and vice versa.

Competence breeds competence and incompetence breeds incompetence. You have to decide every minute of every day which way you are going.

Otherwise, you will be defeating your own possibilities.

PART V

Our journey together has been long, and arduous. Not as long and arduous as actually making a competent organization will be. But a good introduction of what will be required.

The following chapter will be our last stop on this journey. It is all about telling your story, the story of your organization, from the present on to its destiny.

On the last page of chapter one of his book, *Tell to Win*, Peter Guber offers the wisdom of his long and successful career by offering for our preliminary understanding the following:

"aHHa!

- *Move your listeners' hearts, and their feet and [minds] will follow.*
- *Data dumps are not stories—dump them, don't tell them!*
- *Story isn't the icing on the cake, it **is** the cake.*
- *Don't leave home without it . . . your story, that is."*

While Guber came mainly from the entertainment business (for example, as chairman and CEO of SONY Pictures), he knows how to lead an organization. His story is about how to connect and persuade. It is thus fundamental to all leadership.

History is a story, seen from a present point of view. The future is a story, seen from the assumed realities of the present. The present connects the past with the future. It is the critical story.

How you tell it determines in large part how it unfolds, and how it ends. Every organization tells a story. It is a story of what happened to it, buffeted as it was by belief and reality. Or, it is the story of why it was invented and how it is going to get from here to there.

That story gets authored every minute of every day. It is Carlzon's "moments of truth" that create the story and move it forward.

The leader's role in making a competent organization is making its story irresistible and *inevitable*. It is the leader's ultimate tool for success.

"When I was younger, I could remember anything, whether it happened or not."—Mark Twain

19. What's Your *Story?*

Humans emerged in the oral tradition of story-telling. Our nascent brains were molded there. We live our lives embedded in stories. We tell stories to explain ourselves. We tell stories to explain the world we live in. Our lives *are* themselves stories. Our identities as people come from the stories we concoct to provide continuity from our past to our present, and into our future. We belong to them as much as they belong to us.

It is stories that move us. Stories are the source of our laughter and our tears. We do not learn from bare facts. We learn from the stories we invent to explain those facts. Our sense of things comes from our ability to tell—or to consume—stories about them.

We connect with one another via stories. There are love stories. There are war stories. There are stories of sickness and of death, as well as happiness and elation. We live by stories, for stories, and in stories.

Stories are our fundament. They are the power behind feelings. And we are led far more by our feelings than by any reality.

Anne Mulcahy was the CEO who brought Xerox back from near death. This is what she had to say about stories in Gary Burnison's book *No Fear of Failure: Real Stories of How Leaders Deal with Risk and Change*:

> *". . . you have to tell stories that people can relate to and see themselves in and feel a sense of belonging to the organization."*

A good story is one that we can "enter" and participate in. We belong to a tribe or a mob because we feel we are in the same story. The Mafia enjoyed real commitment—sometimes at risk of life. This dedication came from the stories that were shared about the exclusivity of the brotherhood and its legendary heroes.

In America, we are connected in a much weaker way by the legends of our heroes—our George Washingtons, our Paul Bunyans, our "Uncle Sam" and our cowboy heroes. We live off of our myths, which are stories we tell about our past and our present. There is more myth than reality in the JFK we all know.

We seem reticent to make a myth of our ongoing organizations and their heroes. Given how powerful this can be in providing its members with a collective consciousness (and conscience), one wonders . . . why?

When people get together, they swap stories. These are personal stories or stories they have heard or read (gossip). Or, they are stories they make up for some purpose of their own.

For most people most of the time, stories have two implicit purposes:

- To create or solidify the meaning of things in people's lives, to give or maintain some ongoing form to their lives, or to make up explanations of things that seem plausible; and/or
- To create or to solidify the relationships between and among the people who produce or consume them.

Anything that happens in our worlds has to be interpreted. It is all more or less ambiguous. We want to know why the boss is cranky. We want to know why Mary is so secretive. We want to know who's going to get promoted and who's going to get fired. We want to know what size our raise is going to be.

As we have seen, this is simply because nothing we observe comes to us with its meaning inscribed on its back. We could do this for ourselves. But it seems much more factual when a bunch of us share the same interpretations.

In organizations, people are constantly trying to discern the *meaning* of things that occur within or around their organization. The scholar/ writer Karl E. Weick refers to this in the title of his book as *Sensemaking in Organizations*. There may be a whole chain of conversations involving people who are trying to arrive at some collective "sense" of what is going on (or not going on).

Of special interest to any leader is Weick's comment:

> *"Sense may be in the eye of the beholder, but beholders vote and the majority rules."*

He goes on to quote the "pragmatic" psychologist William James (1890) as saying,

> *". . . meanings are considered valid . . . when the consequences of holding them are desirable or useful or good."*

If we add to that the maxim (derived from the sociologist W. I. Thomas) that

If people define a situation as real, it is real in its consequences,

we have a way of understanding just how potent interpretations and explanations are in the life of the organization.

Here is what we can usefully deduce:

- People do not make sense of themselves or their worlds individually. They do so in collaboration with others.
- It is people who make meaning. They "vote" by discussing things.
- Meaning is embedded in plausible stories that people share to explain to themselves whatever needs explaining.
- The criteria are rarely the "truth" or the "facts." If the meaning of something is "desirable or useful or good," we have all of the consensus needed.
- The stories we tell or consume are where we create the truths we cling to. If we define our interpretations (stories) as offering all of the validity we need, they are real in their consequences.

It is the meaning of things—to people or a person—that matters. What you observe or what you believe the facts to be may matter to you. That's because of what they mean *to you*.

Whatever your other tasks may be, the fundamental one is always that of managing meaning (as we considered earlier). Meanings are constructed by people. There is no necessary relationship between what is going on and what people interpret it to mean. Enter the leader. Leaders intervene between the object of conversation and what people interpret it to mean.

You manage meaning in order to have the problems you need, not the ones that just happen to come your way.

The leader is the composer, the orchestrator, and the conductor of what things *should* mean to the people in the organization. The leader makes those meanings plausible, desirable, useful, and good.

The destiny of the organization should always be made to seem inevitable. The meanings that the leader interjects must always support that perspective.

The leader functions as a performing artist. How deft and convincing the leader is in his or her performance determines whether or not those who are members of the organization will willingly suspend their disbelief. That's what great actors, great statesmen, great poets, and great leaders do.

> *When I was still a small child (four years old or so) during the depression, my parents turned me over to my maternal grandparents—with room and board in return for doing my "chores." One of those was drawing water out of the well by bucket to provide the team of horses water in their trough for the hot working day ahead. My attempts to draw the water failed. I had watched my Irish farmer grandfather and knew how to flip the bucket over so it filled with water in the well. But I was not strong enough to bring the bucket up to the top of the well. There was only one way to perform one's chores in those days. And that was to accomplish what needed to be accomplished. No excuses, and no asking for help, since the others had their chores to complete. I had a problem, and*

time was running out. I thought through a half-dozen implausible alternatives. Then I tried something I had never seen done. I filled the bucket half full and could just manage to bring it up. This meant I had to make twice as many trips with the bucket. The horses drank the water from the trough as fast as I could haul it up. I resented their indifference to my predicament. But a chore is a chore, and it is not finished until it is completed. My grandfather had been glancing my way all of this time from afar. He never offered to help. Nor did he offer any advice. He didn't need to say "Good job!" when I finished my chore. Even at four years of age, one is pleased with oneself when a hard job is well done.

I was grateful to him for letting me learn how to do what had to be done. In my view, he became that day a great teacher and a great and caring friend.

There's a story. What does it "say" to you? How will you interpret it—from your point of view . . . or mine . . . or my grandfather's?

From stories, we learn that there is always at least one more perspective than our own from which to view things.

The Danish writer Isak Dinesen (*Out of Africa*) offered this insight:

"To be a person is to have a story to tell."

It is in and through stories that we become who we are. The basic story we have to tell is who we are.

Every leader must ponder this well. People will make a story out of who you are, what you do, and how you do what you do.

The highly-regarded British writer A. S. Byatt wanted us to understand just how basic this story-telling business is:

"Narration (story-telling) is as much a part of human nature as breath and the circulation of the blood.

Every explanation is a story, whether it occurs in a conversation, in the halls and meeting rooms of our organizations, in the theorizing of science, or in art. Like all the rest of human nature, we take doing so for granted. We don't realize what we are doing. We just do it.

As author Annette Simmons put it in her book *The Story Factor*:

> *"We figure out how the world works through the stories we choose to believe. The stories we tell . . . are designed to help us feel like we understand what has happened and why."*

The stories we tell and the stories we believe are the infrastructure of our collective human mind. They may vary from culture to culture. And they certainly vary from organization to organization. But if you want people to join you in a common cause, don't try to reason with them. Tell them a story—the kind of story that will compel them to *belong* to the organization via the story of what it is for and why.

Probably no one in our history was any better at this than Abraham Lincoln, unless it was Mark Twain.

Here's a Lincoln story about how leaders (as in captain of a boat in turbulent waters) sometimes have to be ruthless about performing triage and maintaining focus:

> *"A Virginia farmer once called on President Lincoln and asked to be reimbursed for damage done to his farm by Union soldiers. 'Why, my dear sir,' replied Lincoln. 'If I considered individual cases, I wouldn't have time to get anything done.' But the farmer continued to pester the president until Lincoln finally told this story:*

'You remind me of old Jock Chase, out in Illinois. You see, Jock—I knew him like a brother—used to be a lumberman on the Illinois, and he was steady and sober and the best raftsman on the river. It was quite a trick twenty-five years ago to take the logs over the rapids; but was skillful with a raft and always kept her straight in the channel. Finally, a steamboat was put on, and Jock—he's dead now, poor fellow!—was made captain of her.

One day, when the boat was plunging and wallowing along the boiling current, and Jock's utmost vigilance was being exercised to keep her in the narrow channel, a boy pulled at his coattail and hailed him with, *"Say, mister captain! I wish you would jest stop your boat a minute—I've lost my apple overboard!"*
—from Donald T. Phillips, *Lincoln Stories for Leaders*

Leaders often have people pulling at their coattails for matters of concern to *them*. But the leader has as well a much higher concern—that of the organization's story today and into the future. About his stewardship of the organization as a whole, the leader must sometimes be ruthless. How better than with a story?

This little story also suggests that you do not want anyone on board who does not share that frame of mind. Lincoln was accessible. But he still had his role as chief steward of the organization's interests. And that must always come first.

You might have wondered at one time or another: Why are we so addicted to "the news"? The well-known and widely-respected NBC news anchor Tom Brokaw explains in a comment captured in the Northwestern University *Byline* in the spring of 1982:

> *"It's all storytelling, you know. That's what journalism is all about."*

That's what organizations are all about as well—whether it is between the salesman and a customer, between employees, between employees and their spouses, in meetings, or between the PR people and the public. Storytelling is ubiquitous. It is in managing them and managing their meanings that the leader is challenged and where opportunities arise.

The leader must tell the story of the organization compellingly and as frequently as necessary to displace alternative stories. Why are we here? Why does this organization exist—what is it *for*? Where is it going? What is my role in that journey? Why should I care?

And so on. Stories answer the questions that plague people, but about which they typically have little to say.

THE COMPETENT ORGANIZATION

This perspective on storytelling by leaders is well captured by the novelist John Steinbeck (himself a master storyteller):

> *"We are lonesome animals. We spend all of our life trying to be less lonesome. One of our ancient methods is to tell a story begging the listener to say—and to feel—'Yes, that is the way it is, or at least that is the way I feel it. You're not as alone as you thought.'"*

Great writers have a way of putting things that force us to think out of our comfort zone. Maybe you wouldn't put it that way—"lonesome animals." But it takes only a moment's reflection to realize that we would be totally lonely if we didn't talk to one another. When we do so, we mainly swap stories.

The bond comes when the other person is prompted to think, "Yes, that is the way I feel about it too." We live primarily in the collective consciousness of a set of people. That worldview and the set of beliefs we share are constructed and maintained in communication. And our communication often takes the form of the stories we tell one another.

Steinbeck's last sentence might well have been, for you, "I'm not as alone as I thought." You can meet people and relate to them in the stories that are told and retold.

Stories implicitly serve two other purposes we should pause to consider:

- If you tell any story, you are telling a story about who you are. Who you are gets interpreted by other people to include what you're up to, where you are headed. When you make explicit what is implicit you are making a commitment. You have to live up to your story. Otherwise, people will lose interest. And you will lose credibility. So the stories you tell publicly produce for you a kind of obligation—an obligation to live up to how people interpret your stories. This is a good thing. It makes it necessary for you to fulfill the stories you tell about yourself and your destiny.
- Another implicit but important function of stories has to do with how we treat them. William Carlos Williams was a physician and a poet. He was one of physician/psychiatrist Robert Coles' mentors (as related in his book, *The Call of Stories*). About Williams, Coles wrote:

> *"Continuities and discontinuities, themes that appeared and disappeared, references, comparisons, similes and metaphors, intimations and suggestions, moods and mysteries, contours of coherence and spells of impenetrability—he spoke of such matters as he brooded over his life as a doctor, a writer . . . ."*

In other words, our lives are richer, more complex, more contradictory than any story could tell. Stories give us a glimpse, a snapshot of another person. But the real story is the convoluted life that each person lives.

Who we are is more than we can say. Who another person is, is always more than he or she can say in so many words. We have to be alert, to listen, to learn.

A life is always a life in progress. It is the same with an organization. Unless it is at all times a life in progress, it will suffer from stultification. It will wither and die with no more than a financial reason for being.

It is the leader's task to infuse his or her organization with all the life it can handle. This is done primarily and inadvertently by who the leader IS. That's the real story that people attend to.

But it can be aided and abetted by the stories that the leader tells—about the organization's cause in life, about its destiny, and about how it is going to get there.

The self-effacing (humble, we might say) leader is always welcome, always listened to.

So, a brief story to close this exploration of such an important subject:

> *"As I left Denver to come here today," began a corporate president, "my secretary gave me a few words of encouragement. She said, 'I know you're nervous about addressing the field staff, but don't be intimidated. And don't try to be charming, intellectual, or funny . . . . Just be yourself.'"*

One more (that CEOs seem to enjoy)?

THE COMPETENT ORGANIZATION

The CEO had his arm over his protégé's shoulder. They were standing atop a hill overlooking a beautiful valley. The CEO said "Imagine a huge white house there in the center of that valley. It is surrounded by pools and gardens. In one pasture are wonderfully alert race horses. In another pasture, there are sleek black cattle. Imagine that there are big red barns and a 6-stall garage filled with vintage cars. On one veranda there is a wonderfully-dressed woman and her two children. Can you imagine all that?" "Oh, yes sir, I can," said the eager young man. "Well," said the CEO, "just keep in mind that if you work hard and make our organization successful, then one day all of that could be . . . . MINE!" (probably apocryphal)

Who could resist this one?

When John D. Rockefeller (Sr.) learned that his family had ordered an electric car for his surprise birthday present, which would enable him to get around his vast estate more easily, he commented "If it's all the same to you, I'd rather have the money."

[If you should want to read more about storytelling, I can recommend the following to you:]

Robert Coles, *The Call of Stories (1989)*

Steven Denning, *The Leader's Guide to Storytelling (2005)*

Peter Guber, *Tell to Win (2011)*

Donald T. Phillips, *Lincoln Stories for Leaders (1997)*

Annette Simmons, *The Story Factor (2001)*

20. Afterword

In this book I have tried to share with you what I have learned over a lifetime of work with CEOs, presidents, politicians and commanders, partnering with them in making sustainably competent (or even virtuoso) organizations. I have been involved with all kinds of organizations in the U. S. and very different cultures around the world.

In the early years, there were no road signs. It was uncharted territory. We often had to make it up as we went along. It was a bit like trying to learn how to play the violin when the concert was already underway.

There was nothing easy about this either for me or for the courageous leaders who ventured into these daunting endeavors. We decided upon what we were trying to achieve at the nitty-gritty level. Then we had to invent a way of getting there—of making it happen. Then we had to measure our progress.

Most of what I have learned of importance about making competent organizations I have learned from being "in the trenches" with the person in charge and his or her people making it happen. I carried with me as much of the world's wisdom as I could comprehend. In other words, I had already done my "homework." One should not go into alien territory without the best provisions for the adventure.

I make no claim that this is the only way of doing it. It has been full of stunning challenges. But it is for me a way of understanding deeply what has to be done. And then of figuring out how to do it.

If I were to recount what my clients and I have learned in these expeditions into the relative unknown, this book would be ten times this size. I have instead tried to distill the best of what we have learned over the past fifty years or so into a manageable, readable, and implementable book.

If all of the preceding helps you in some small way to make your organization more competent, or to make yourself as *the* leader more competent, this book will have fulfilled its purpose.

If you have a comment or a question, email me: *lee.thayer@att.net*. I'm still learning. If you are, who knows what we might accomplish together?

In any event, I salute you who stay on or get pulled into the trenches. You have the toughest, most challenging job on the planet.

Consider this book your field guide. If it is a more competent organization that you aim for, you will find much here that is of value for one primary reason: *it works*.

Let it work for you.

*   *   *

> *"It is an immutable law in business that words are words, explanations are explanations, promises are promises—but only performance is reality."*
> —Harold S. Geneen

Dedication and Acknowledgements

This book is dedicated to the few truly competent people I have come across in my lifetime. They are few compared to the hundreds who have crossed your path and mine.

They must remain anonymous. They were not *trying* to be competent just to impress me. They were competent as a result of the habits they had developed over the years. They just couldn't help it.

Neither can the incompetents and marginally-competent folks who people our planet. It has simply become habitual for them, and they get paid for it (or are forgiven in our hyper-liberal society) anyway. We have permitted them to remain dependent adolescents for life. It's our fault.

As the German poet and philosopher Goethe said,

> *We should love people not for what they are, but for what they could be.*

We apparently do not know how to do that. Our general orientation toward "unconditional love" has ruined millions. That's a shame.

But perhaps all the more reasons for saluting the few truly competent people who come along. They are the only hope we have.

There have been hundreds of authors who preceded me down this prickly path. They understood the problem. But they had no way of solving it.

Like them, I understand the problem. But, like them, mine may be as well a cry in the wilderness of modern society,

Truly competent people in all walks of life will applaud my attempts here. Incompetent people don't read books such as this—or at least they shun those that do not endorse the comfort zone they are in.

I thank my readers who "get it." I feel sorry for those who don't, for by sheer numbers they are the future.

In the work I do with CEOs—making extraordinary organizations out of ordinary ones—we convert those people . . . one by one.

Appendix A

The rationale and framework for **Role Descriptions** were set forth in chapters 12 and 13. If you need to refresh your memory regarding those, please do so.

The first part of the role description is intended to set forth in a series of brief bullets what the incumbent of the role would learn to accomplish—*under adversity*—3 to 6 years hence. The assumption is that people would learn how to perform their roles better today than they did yesterday. The purpose of the role description is to set the *directions* of their growth and enhanced performance. Examples of how you might do this are provided below.

The second part of the role description—**Performance Goals**—set forth the immediate and mid-term accomplishments for the person in that role. They must be objectively measurable (measurable by anyone) and on a specific timeline. These are organization-specific and therefore offer no generic examples.

The third part of the role description—the **Learning Plan**—addresses the agreed-upon (between superior and subordinate) shortfalls on the part of the role incumbent. These may be matters of attitude, knowledge, skills, or failure to grow in place. Collaboratively, the two persons arrive at a specific course of action, with specified accomplishments—again on a timeline. Again, these are person-specific. Examples could be misleading.

Below are examples of generic role descriptions so you can see how they might be done.

[*What is very important is that both persons have the same understanding of every item and of every word. It is this deliberation that is agreed upon. The subordinate then takes the document (which is just for the purpose of validating what they have discussed) and makes crude plans for accomplishing each bullet on the role description. The subordinate would also offer up plans for their performance goals and learning plan. The superior signs off on the **plan**. This is where the commitment and the covenant between them comes from.*]

{Reminder: It isn't the document that matters. It is the face-to-face collaborative discussions between superior and subordinate that matter. And the role description can be improved upon at any time by mutual consent.]

Role Description—**Receptionist**

- My role: To make XYZ organization the best in the business by any measure
- By never permitting a caller or visitor to *wonder*
- By becoming the *voice* and the personality of this organization
- By recognizing frequent callers by name
- By knowing at all times where every key person in this organization is, whether they know it or not
- By developing the most sophisticated, reliable systems there could be connecting the people who ought to be connected, and keeping unconnected those who ought not be connected
- By inventing and developing the best administrative support systems in the business, giving us sustainable competitive advantage
- By making every caller's or visitor's day
- By becoming a virtuoso question-asker
- By having at all times a person who could take over my role and do it better than I do
- By knowing the names and the roles in all of our customers', our suppliers', and our competitors' organizations
- By becoming the best in the business in my role in terms of public acclamation

Role Description—**Business-Maker**

My role: To make XYZ organization the best in the business by any measure

[Every commercial organization has "profit centers." Every NFP has people engaged in gathering funding. Some organizations have salespeople. These can all be agglomerated under the rubric of "business-makers."]

- By developing myself (salesperson or sales-engineer) and/or my business unit into the best in the business by any measure
- By leading in the generation of performance numbers that significantly exceed those of this or any comparable industry
- By recruiting, selecting, and developing the right people in all of the right roles (if you have subordinates)
- By leading the invention, reinvention, and reliable implementation of the most innovative, highest-quality, most cost-effective processes in the world
- By leading in the creation of a culture in which there are only two categories: those who serve the customers (clients) directly, and those who serve those who are serving the customers
- By developing an organization structure in which every role has "customers" in other roles
- By providing a real-time performance feedback system that recognizes first team performance, and only then individual performance
- By putting myself and all others around me in the learning mode
- By having at all times at least one person who is ready, willing, and able to take over my role and perform it better than I do

Role description—**Leader: Performance Resources**

(sometimes referred to as Human Resources)

My role: To make XYZ organization the best in the business by any measure

- By applying evolutionary and revolutionary thinking to envision and enable what this organization should become
- By proactively communicating that thinking to the leaders of this organization, the Board, and the entire staff in a way that excites and motivated them to commit to the journey
- By critically assessing the vision to identify organization development opportunities that would facilitate the fulfillment of the vision
- By establishing, in collaboration with the members of the organization learning plans for every member—including the CEO and other leaders
- By personifying the learning mode in this organization and throughout the industry
- By becoming the "go-to" source for all learning and developmental needs
- By leading in the process of members' growth and performance, and inventing world-class systems for doing so
- By learning how to assist any and all of our stakeholders (including our competitors) in raising the performance of their people and their organizations
- By becoming the chief spokesperson for the XYZ-way here and abroad
- By becoming the exemplary steward of this organization's conscience and its destiny
- By having ready, willing, and able at least one person who could take over my role and perform it better than I do

Role Description—**Project Team Leader**

My role: To make XYZ organization the best in the business by any measure

- By **composing** the project team—people and systems—in such a way that the performance goals of the team are exceeded on every occasion
- By **leading** the team and all of its members to become virtuoso performers
- By **providing**—directly or indirectly—all of the wherewithal required for raising performance on a daily basis
- By **coordinating**, through superlative strategic and tactical communication, the efforts and needs of the team
- By **knowing** thoroughly what bears upon the performance of the team and its individual members—thus anticipating and deflecting most problems
- By **developing** the kinds of visual, spatial, and temporal measurements of exactly where the project is and where it has yet to go, in terms of **variance**
- By **equipping** team members to take the lead in fixing 80-90% of the variance when it occurs on the critical path—thus minimizing the need for "meetings"
- By **doing** what has to be done to enable every member to lead, follow, or get out of the way
- By **mentoring** the next generation of team leaders to perform better than the present set

Role Description—**CEO** or **President**

My role: To make XYZ organization the best in the business by any measure

- By ensuring (by any or all means required) the financial/economic health, welfare, growth, and security of this organization
- By making sure that the right people are on the right bus and in the right seat, and requiring the same of all of the other leaders of this organization
- By making certain that the bus is always headed in the right direction
- By making this organization into the kind of place where the *best* (most competent) people want to work
- By making certain that our leaders are the main reason why the best people want to be here
- Having a national reputation for being the best maker of "Business Makers" in the country
- By being the most articulate spokesperson for our mission, inside and outside the organization
- By establishing what are considered to be impossible goals—*and equipping people to achieve them*
- By exceeding the needs and aspirations of all of our stakeholders
- By becoming the role model for learning, growth, and change
- By becoming the chief steward of this organization's cause in life, and having apprentice stewards at every level
- By having at all times at least one person ready, willing, and able to take over my role and perform it better than I do

Role Description—**COO (Operations)**

My role: To make XYZ organization the best in the business by any measure

- By continuously re-designing the systems and processes of the operating infrastructure of this organization so that (a) we are always optimizing the pursuit of our mission, (b) all of the performance goals of every person and every unit can be exceeded, and (c) our customers or clients will never have reason to consider any alternative
- By providing world-class logistics for information, product or services, and for timely and error-free movement of anything that bears upon our performance
- By putting everything operational together in such a way that the yield from direct and indirect costs is optimum
- By becoming widely recognized as setting the bar for operational excellence and innovation
- By making certain that the operating teams or individuals throughout the organization are the best informed, most capable, most highly-empowered, and most rightly composed in this or any comparable industry
- By having at least one person ready, willing, and able to take over my role and perform it better than I do

[These are but examples. But they may suggest how to go about creating role descriptions that can always be measured by accomplishments—whether explicit or implicit. The exercise of collaboratively creating a role description for any role in the organization is in itself very enlightening—worth doing.]

Appendix B

[More on "**Our Guiding Values and Beliefs**." The first page of such a document appears in Chapter 15. It is headed:

We believe that good work, superbly done, is the richest source of human dignity and of quality of life

What follows on each page of such a document is a succinct heading with a few lines explicating what that is supposed to mean to everyone in the organization. This particular entry is followed by an "unpacking" on the following page.

These values and beliefs are primarily those of the chief executive of the organization. The exercise of arriving at a priority set of values and beliefs is of great import for that executive, whether published or not.

Three reminders:

- These are not any organization's present values and beliefs. They are the ones to be aspired to by every member.
- This is a working document. It can be modified, added to or subtracted from at any time. Every leader in the organization must exemplify these values and beliefs, and should observe any shortfalls anywhere in the organization on an everyday basis.
- These are, indeed, ideals. But if you don't aim for the ideal, your aim is wrong.

[What follows are sample pages. Each value and belief should be presented on one page or less.]

We believe that the world passes by those who do not change with it.

- History is replete with stories of companies and nations which have failed because they didn't evolve with the times. And people: even the most educated often become obsolete because they were trying to get by on one year's experience repeated over and over again.
- People may blame their troubles on something or someone else. But if people don't learn and grow, they may fail. A failed organization can make no more than negative contributions to the lives of its members. We all have a compelling need to keep our organization healthy.
- Change requires courage. And it requires a sense of life as an exciting journey. Those who refuse to make that journey may be stuck for the rest of their lives where they *were.*
- Growth and the changes that come with it are natural. Young children are the most alive. That's because of the pace of their learning, and their involvement in what's going on. They are in the "learning mode," If you are not, you will miss the best part of life.
- If we change together, we all win together. If we don't, we may all lose.

We believe that a *question* from which we might learn is superior to any old knowledge that we try to apply to new things.

- Fresh questions grow us. Stale answers stagnate us.
- Answers are like brakes. We don't become smarter by knowing all the answers.
- Learning how to ask just the right question at the right time may be the ultimate human competence.
- With problems in the real world, there is no 2 + 2 = 4. That happens only in *closed* systems. The world we deal with is an open system. We have to be open to it. We have to struggle against falling into the "knowing mode."
- It is the quality of the questions a person puts to himself or herself that enables that person to learn from the questions asked of others.

- Questions lead us. Answers trap us. The right question opens up new possibilities. To be what we want to be requires us to live in the world of possibilities, not the world of yesterday's answers.
- Questions create new pathways. The same old answers keep us in the rut.

We believe in saying what we mean, and meaning what we say.

- We believe that people should be responsible for the *consequences* of what they do or do not say.
- Before we speak or write, we should consider carefully what we *mean* by what we say. We intend to lead others to what we mean by what we say as directly as possible.
- We believe that those who receive our communication are as responsible as we are for understanding what we *mean* by what we say.
- We believe that the final responsibility for understanding what others *mean* by what they say or do is the receiver's. We intend to avoid assumptions by asking what was meant.
- We believe that the consequences of misinterpreting or misunderstanding what others mean by what they say belong to the person who misinterprets or misunderstands.
- We believe that people who do not mean what they say are responsible for the consequences.
- Muddy communication directly reflects muddy thinking. A person may not be responsible for others' misinterpretations, but is responsible for muddy or careless thinking.

We believe that agreements or promises not fulfilled amount to lying or deceit, minimally to unwarranted problems.

- If there is a possibility that we are going to fail to keep our commitments or promises—for whatever reasons—we believe we should announce this as far in advance as possible, preferably before making the commitment.
- We believe that if we are not competent to do something requested, we should say so.

- We believe that trust hinges upon our saying what we mean and meaning what we say—being trustworthy. We believe our word is our seal.

We believe that people are the masters of their own destiny.

- If they are not, then someone or something else would be. We believe this is shirking one's primary responsibility—to oneself.
- We believe that people are responsible for getting themselves into the right role in the right organization. We do not believe that people are interchangeable pawns.
- In order to avoid the problems this causes, we must all know what we want to be when we grow up, and be daily committed to that growing-up. This should not be left to others to decide.
- A competent organization is an organization of grown-ups. We believe that the more dependent people are, the more dependent the organization is on outside forces for its own condition and destiny.
- We believe that if the organization does not control its own destiny, some competitor or economic condition will.
- We believe therefore that people who cannot be trusted to be responsible for their own lives cannot be trusted to be responsible for others' lives. They cannot be fully-qualified members of this organization.
- The more responsibility people take for their own lives, the more freedom and choices you expect to have at work.
- We believe that competence is the mother of what you can expect to gain or lose at work.
- We believe that people who are not committed to empowering themselves cannot be rightly empowered.
- We believe that people who are growing are growing in relevance, and that those who are not growing are declining in relevance—to themselves and to this organization.
- We believe that every member owns that problem. The organization does not.

[Try your hand at "unpacking" the next three along the lines of the preceding.]

We believe that people who are not living with some purpose greater than their own are living impoverished lives.

LEE THAYER

We believe in paying people for the increases in competence in their roles, and for their accomplishments, not their activities or credentials or position or "seniority."

We believe in civility, in good manners, and in propriety.

You will be able to think of others, of course. The important thing is not the document. The important thing is that anyone who visits your organization, or joins it, would be able to quickly deduce the organization's values and beliefs by how all of the members comport themselves on a daily basis.

CPSIA information can be obtained at www.ICGtesting.com
Printed in the USA
LVOW06s1654010814

397112LV00003B/467/P